AZURE DEVOPS ENGINEER EXAM AZ-400

DESIGNING AND IMPLEMENTING MICROSOFT DEVOPS SOLUTIONS

4 BOOKS IN 1

BOOK 1
AZURE DEVOPS FUNDAMENTALS: A BEGINNER'S GUIDE TO EXAM AZ-400

BOOK 2
MASTERING CONTINUOUS INTEGRATION AND CONTINUOUS DEPLOYMENT WITH AZURE DEVOPS: EXAM AZ-400

BOOK 3
ADVANCED AZURE DEVOPS TECHNIQUES: ARCHITECTING FOR SCALABILITY AND RESILIENCE - EXAM AZ-400

BOOK 4
DEVOPS EXPERT: ACHIEVING MASTERY IN AZURE DEVOPS AND BEYOND - EXAM AZ-400

ROB BOTWRIGHT

Published by Rob Botwright
Library of Congress Cataloging-in-Publication Data
ISBN 978-1-83938-680-0
Cover design by Rizzo

Disclaimer

The contents of this book are based on extensive research and the best available historical sources. However, the author and publisher make no claims, promises, or guarantees about the accuracy, completeness, or adequacy of the information contained herein. The information in this book is provided on an "as is" basis, and the author and publisher disclaim any and all liability for any errors, omissions, or inaccuracies in the information or for any actions taken in reliance on such information. The opinions and views expressed in this book are those of the author and do not necessarily reflect the official policy or position of any organization or individual mentioned in this book. Any reference to specific people, places, or events is intended only to provide historical context and is not intended to defame or malign any group, individual, or entity. The information in this book is intended for educational and entertainment purposes only. It is not intended to be a substitute for professional advice or judgment. Readers are encouraged to conduct their own research and to seek professional advice where appropriate. Every effort has been made to obtain necessary permissions and acknowledgments for all images and other copyrighted material used in this book. Any errors or omissions in this regard are unintentional, and the author and publisher will correct them in future editions.

BOOK 1 - AZURE DEVOPS FUNDAMENTALS: A BEGINNER'S GUIDE TO EXAM AZ-400

BOOK 2 - MASTERING CONTINUOUS INTEGRATION AND CONTINUOUS DEPLOYMENT WITH AZURE DEVOPS: EXAM AZ-400

BOOK 3 - ADVANCED AZURE DEVOPS TECHNIQUES: ARCHITECTING FOR SCALABILITY AND RESILIENCE - EXAM AZ-400

BOOK 4 - DEVOPS EXPERT: ACHIEVING MASTERY IN AZURE DEVOPS AND BEYOND - EXAM AZ-400

Introduction

Welcome to the comprehensive book bundle "Azure DevOps Engineer: Exam AZ-400 - Designing and Implementing Microsoft DevOps Solutions." In today's rapidly evolving technological landscape, the demand for skilled DevOps professionals continues to grow exponentially. To meet this demand and excel in the field of DevOps, individuals must possess a deep understanding of Azure DevOps and the ability to design and implement robust DevOps solutions.

This book bundle is designed to provide readers with a holistic journey through the world of Azure DevOps, covering fundamental concepts, advanced techniques, and expert strategies necessary to succeed as a DevOps engineer. Whether you are new to Azure DevOps or seeking to advance your skills to the next level, this bundle offers a comprehensive learning experience tailored to your needs.

Book 1 - Azure DevOps Fundamentals: A Beginner's Guide to Exam AZ-400, serves as the starting point for individuals embarking on their DevOps journey. This book introduces readers to the core concepts of Azure DevOps, laying a solid foundation for further exploration into the world of DevOps.

Book 2 - Mastering Continuous Integration and Continuous Deployment with Azure DevOps: Exam AZ-400, dives deep into the realm of CI/CD pipelines, guiding readers through the process of automating software delivery using Azure DevOps. By mastering CI/CD techniques, readers will learn how to accelerate software delivery, improve quality, and enhance collaboration within their teams.

Book 3 - Advanced Azure DevOps Techniques: Architecting for Scalability and Resilience - Exam AZ-400, explores advanced topics such as scalability, resilience, and architectural patterns in Azure DevOps. Through real-world case studies and practical examples, readers will gain the knowledge and skills needed to design and implement scalable and resilient DevOps solutions.

Book 4 - DevOps Expert: Achieving Mastery in Azure DevOps and Beyond - Exam AZ-400, serves as the ultimate guide for individuals striving to become true experts in Azure DevOps. Covering a wide range of advanced topics, this book empowers readers to tackle complex challenges with confidence and proficiency.

Together, these four books offer a comprehensive roadmap for individuals aspiring to become Azure DevOps engineers. Whether you are preparing for the AZ-400 exam or seeking to advance your career in DevOps, this book bundle will equip you with the knowledge, skills, and strategies needed to succeed in today's fast-paced, technology-driven world.

BOOK 1
AZURE DEVOPS FUNDAMENTALS
A BEGINNER'S GUIDE TO EXAM AZ-400

ROB BOTWRIGHT

Chapter 1: Introduction to Azure DevOps

Understanding DevOps principles is essential for anyone involved in software development and operations. DevOps is not just a set of practices but a cultural shift in the way teams collaborate and deliver software. At its core, DevOps emphasizes collaboration, automation, and continuous improvement. Teams practicing DevOps aim to break down silos between development and operations, fostering a culture of shared responsibility and accountability.

One of the key principles of DevOps is automation, where repetitive tasks are automated to streamline processes and reduce manual errors. Continuous integration (CI) is another fundamental DevOps principle, where developers frequently integrate their code into a shared repository, triggering automated builds and tests. Continuous delivery (CD) extends CI by automating the deployment process, ensuring that software can be reliably deployed to production at any time. Infrastructure as code (IaC) is a DevOps practice where infrastructure is managed through code, allowing for consistency, scalability, and version control. Monitoring and feedback are crucial in DevOps, enabling teams to detect and respond to issues quickly, improving overall system reliability. DevOps also promotes a blameless culture, where failures are viewed as learning opportunities rather than finger-pointing exercises. Tools such as Docker and Kubernetes have become integral to DevOps practices, enabling containerization and orchestration of applications for scalability and portability. Collaboration tools like Slack and Microsoft Teams facilitate communication and knowledge sharing among DevOps teams. Embracing DevOps principles requires a mindset shift and continuous learning, as technologies and practices evolve rapidly in the ever-changing landscape of software development.

In practice, adopting DevOps often involves breaking down organizational silos and fostering cross-functional teams that work together towards common goals. Continuous integration pipelines, configured using tools like Jenkins or Azure DevOps, automate the build, test, and integration process, enabling faster feedback loops and higher quality software. Infrastructure as code tools such as Terraform or Ansible enable teams to provision and manage infrastructure using code, ensuring consistency and repeatability across environments. Monitoring tools like Prometheus or Datadog provide insights into application performance and health, allowing teams to proactively address issues before they impact users. DevOps principles are not limited to technology; they also encompass cultural aspects such as collaboration, communication, and empathy. By embracing DevOps principles, organizations can achieve faster time-to-market, improved reliability, and better alignment with customer needs. Continuous learning and improvement are core tenets of DevOps, as teams strive to optimize processes and adapt to changing requirements and technologies. Overall, understanding and embodying DevOps principles is essential for modern software development teams looking to thrive in today's fast-paced and competitive landscape.

The evolution of Azure DevOps traces back to the early days of Microsoft's foray into software development and collaboration tools. Initially, Microsoft offered standalone products like Visual SourceSafe and Team Foundation Server (TFS) to address version control and application lifecycle management needs. However, as the software development landscape evolved, so did the requirements for collaboration and DevOps practices. In response to these changing needs, Microsoft introduced Azure DevOps, a comprehensive suite of tools and services designed to facilitate collaboration, automation, and continuous delivery in software development. Azure DevOps encompasses a range of services, including Azure Repos for version control, Azure Pipelines for continuous integration and deployment, Azure Boards for project management, Azure Artifacts for package management, and Azure Test Plans for testing and quality assurance. This integrated suite of tools allows development teams to plan, build, test, deploy, and monitor software applications seamlessly.

One of the key milestones in the evolution of Azure DevOps was the transition from TFS to Azure DevOps Services, a cloud-based offering that provides scalable and flexible infrastructure for development teams. Azure DevOps Services offers built-in integration with Azure cloud services, enabling teams to leverage the power of the cloud for their development and deployment workflows. Another significant development in the evolution of Azure DevOps was the introduction of Azure Pipelines, a powerful CI/CD solution that supports building, testing, and deploying applications across multiple platforms and environments. With Azure Pipelines, teams can define their build and release pipelines as code using YAML or a visual designer, allowing for versioning, collaboration, and automation of the entire software delivery process. Additionally, Azure Pipelines offers extensive integration capabilities with popular development platforms, version control systems, and third-party services, making it a versatile and adaptable solution for modern DevOps workflows. The adoption of DevOps practices and tools like Azure DevOps has become increasingly prevalent in organizations of all sizes and industries. This shift is driven by the need for faster time-to-market, improved quality, and increased collaboration among development, operations, and quality assurance teams. Azure DevOps provides a unified platform for teams to collaborate on software projects, manage their codebase, automate build and release processes, and track progress using agile project management techniques.

Moreover, Azure DevOps integrates seamlessly with other Microsoft services and tools, such as Visual Studio, Azure Active Directory, and Microsoft Teams, further enhancing productivity and collaboration for development teams. The evolution of Azure DevOps reflects Microsoft's commitment to empowering developers and organizations with modern, cloud-native tools and services for software development and delivery. As technology continues to evolve and organizations embrace digital transformation, Azure DevOps is poised to remain a central component of the DevOps toolchain, enabling teams to innovate and deliver value to customers faster and more *efficiently than ever before. In summary, the evolution of Azure DevOps represents a significant milestone in the journey towards modern software development practices and underscores Microsoft's dedication to providing cutting-edge solutions for developers and organizations worldwide.*

Chapter 2: Understanding Version Control Systems

Git, a distributed version control system, has become the cornerstone of modern software development workflows. It revolutionized the way developers collaborate, track changes, and manage codebases across distributed teams. Understanding the fundamentals of Git is essential for any developer looking to navigate the complexities of version control effectively. At its core, Git provides a robust framework for managing changes to codebases, enabling developers to work collaboratively on projects with confidence. The primary concept in Git is the repository, which serves as a central storehouse for code and project history. To create a new Git repository, developers can use the git init command in their project directory, initializing a new repository locally. Once a repository is initialized, developers can start adding files and directories to the project and tracking changes using Git. The git add command is used to stage changes for commit, selecting which modifications to include in the next commit snapshot. After staging changes, developers can commit them to the repository using the git commit command, along with a descriptive commit message summarizing the changes made. Commits in Git represent snapshots of the project at a specific point in time, allowing developers to track the evolution of their codebase over time. Git also provides powerful branching and merging capabilities, enabling developers to work on multiple features or bug fixes concurrently without interfering with each other's progress. The git branch command allows developers to create, list, and manage branches in the repository, while the git checkout command allows them to switch between branches seamlessly. Branches in Git provide a lightweight mechanism for isolating work in progress, facilitating collaborative development workflows. When a feature or bug fix is complete, developers can merge their changes back into the main branch using the git merge command, integrating their work with the rest of the project. Git's branching and merging model promotes parallel development and enables teams to collaborate effectively on complex projects. Additionally, Git provides robust mechanisms for tracking and reverting changes, helping developers recover from mistakes or unexpected issues quickly. The git log command allows developers to view the commit history of the repository, inspecting the changes made by themselves and other contributors. In situations where changes need to be undone, Git offers the git revert and git reset commands, allowing developers to revert commits or reset the repository to a previous state. Git also supports remote repositories, enabling distributed collaboration among team members working in different locations. The git remote command facilitates interactions with remote repositories, such as pushing changes to a shared repository or fetching updates from a remote server. By leveraging remote repositories, developers can collaborate seamlessly on projects and share code with colleagues across the globe. GitHub, a popular hosting service for Git repositories, further enhances collaboration and code sharing by providing additional features such as pull requests, issue tracking, and project management tools. By integrating Git with platforms like GitHub, developers can streamline their workflows and enhance productivity in collaborative software development projects. In summary, Git fundamentals encompass a range of concepts and commands that empower developers to manage codebases effectively, collaborate with team members, and track changes with confidence. As developers continue to adopt Git as their version control system of choice, understanding its fundamentals becomes increasingly important for success in modern software development environments. Whether working on solo projects or contributing to large-scale open-source initiatives, mastering Git fundamentals lays the foundation for efficient and collaborative software development *practices.*

Branching strategies play a pivotal role in the success of software development projects, providing structure and organization to collaborative workflows. At their core, branching strategies define how developers manage concurrent streams of work within a codebase, facilitating parallel development and enabling teams to work on multiple features or bug fixes simultaneously. One of the most widely adopted branching strategies is the Gitflow workflow, which organizes development into distinct branches for feature development, release preparation, and hotfixes. In Gitflow, the main branches include master, representing the stable production-ready code, and develop, serving as the integration branch for ongoing development work. Feature branches are created off the develop branch and merged back once the feature is complete, ensuring that new functionality is thoroughly tested and integrated before release. Additionally, Gitflow defines release branches for preparing new releases and hotfix branches for addressing critical issues in production. This structured approach to branching promotes stability, traceability, and collaboration across development teams. Another common branching strategy is the GitHub Flow, which emphasizes simplicity and continuous delivery. In GitHub Flow, all development work is performed directly on the master branch, with feature branches created as needed for specific tasks. Developers collaborate on feature branches, submitting pull requests to merge their changes into the master branch once they are ready for review and deployment. Continuous integration and automated testing are integral to the GitHub Flow, ensuring that changes are thoroughly validated before being merged into the main branch. This lightweight branching model fosters rapid iteration and encourages a culture of experimentation and innovation. A third branching strategy, known as the Trunk-Based Development, advocates for a minimalist approach to branching, with all development occurring on a single main branch. In Trunk-Based Development, developers commit changes directly to the main branch, relying on feature flags and toggles to isolate unfinished work and control feature visibility. Continuous integration and deployment pipelines play a crucial role in Trunk-Based Development, automating testing and deployment processes to ensure that changes are rapidly validated and released. While Trunk-Based Development offers simplicity and agility, it requires careful coordination and discipline to avoid conflicts and maintain code quality. Ultimately, the choice of branching strategy depends on various factors, including team size, project complexity, and organizational culture. Some teams may prefer the structure and predictability of Gitflow, while others *may opt for the flexibility and speed of GitHub Flow or Trunk-Based Development. Regardless of the chosen strategy, effective collaboration, communication, and automation are essential for success. Modern version control systems and collaboration platforms provide robust support for branching workflows, offering features such as pull requests, code reviews, and automated testing to streamline development processes. By embracing best practices and leveraging the capabilities of these tools, development teams can navigate the complexities of branching strategies with confidence and deliver high-quality software efficiently. In summary, branching strategies are a foundational aspect of software development, shaping how teams collaborate, iterate, and deliver value to their users. Whether following established models like Gitflow or embracing more lightweight approaches like GitHub Flow or Trunk-Based Development, choosing the right branching strategy is crucial for achieving success in today's fast-paced and dynamic development environments.*

Chapter 3: Setting Up Your First Azure DevOps Project

Creating projects and repositories is a fundamental aspect of setting up a successful software development environment. In modern development workflows, projects serve as containers for organizing related codebases, documentation, and collaboration tools. To create a new project, developers can leverage a variety of platforms and tools, such as GitHub, GitLab, Bitbucket, or Azure DevOps. Each platform offers its unique set of features and integrations, catering to different preferences and requirements. The process of creating a project typically begins by logging into the chosen platform and navigating to the dashboard or homepage. From there, developers can initiate the project creation process by selecting the "New Project" or "Create Project" option. Depending on the platform, developers may be prompted to provide essential project details, such as the project name, description, and visibility settings. Once the project details are entered, developers can proceed to create the project, triggering the provisioning of resources and setting up the project environment. After creating the project, the next step is to set up the repository, which serves as the central storehouse for the project's source code and version history. To create a new repository, developers can navigate to the project's repository section and select the "New Repository" or "Create Repository" option. They may then be prompted to specify the repository name, description, and other configuration settings, such as the repository visibility and access controls. Once the repository details are entered, developers can proceed to create the repository, initializing it with an initial commit containing a README file or other project artifacts. With the repository created, developers can then clone it to their local development environment using the git clone command, enabling them to start working on the project locally. Alternatively, developers can push existing codebases to the newly created repository using the git push command, initializing the repository with their project's codebase. As development progresses, developers can collaborate on the project by pushing and pulling changes to and from the remote repository, ensuring that everyone is working with the latest version of the code. Additionally, platforms like GitHub and GitLab offer features such as pull requests and code reviews, enabling developers to review and discuss changes before merging them into the main codebase. This collaborative workflow promotes transparency, code quality, and knowledge sharing among team members. In addition to source code, repositories can also contain other project assets, such as documentation, configuration files, and build scripts, further enhancing the project's organization and accessibility. By creating projects and repositories effectively, developers lay the foundation for successful collaboration, innovation, and delivery in software development projects. Whether working on open-source initiatives, enterprise projects, or personal endeavors, mastering the process of creating projects and repositories is essential for navigating the complexities of modern development workflows. In summary, creating projects and repositories is a critical step in establishing a productive and organized development environment, enabling teams to collaborate effectively and deliver high-quality software efficiently.

Configuring project settings is an essential task for tailoring the development environment to specific project requirements and preferences. In modern software development platforms like GitHub, GitLab, Bitbucket, or Azure DevOps, project settings encompass a wide range of options and configurations that impact how teams collaborate, manage codebases, and track project progress. To access project settings, developers typically navigate to the project dashboard or settings page, where they can configure various aspects of the project's behavior and appearance. One of the primary settings developers may adjust is the project's name and description, providing a clear and descriptive overview of the project's purpose and goals. Additionally, developers can configure the project's visibility settings, specifying whether it should be public, private, or accessible to specific users or teams. This setting helps control who can view, clone, and contribute to the project, ensuring that sensitive information remains secure and accessible only to authorized individuals. Another crucial aspect of project settings is the collaboration and access control settings, which define how team members interact with the project and its resources. Platforms like GitHub and GitLab offer granular access control features, allowing project owners to define roles, permissions, and access levels for team members. This ensures that everyone has the appropriate level of access to project repositories, issues, and other project assets. Project settings also include configuration options for integrating third-party services and tools, such as continuous integration (CI) pipelines, issue trackers, and project management tools. By integrating these services seamlessly into the project workflow, developers can automate repetitive tasks, streamline collaboration, and improve overall productivity. For example, in Azure DevOps, developers can configure

CI/CD pipelines directly within the project settings, defining build and release workflows to automate the deployment process. Similarly, platforms like GitHub and GitLab offer integrations with popular CI/CD tools like Jenkins, Travis CI, and CircleCI, enabling teams to leverage their preferred tools and services seamlessly. Additionally, project settings often include options for configuring issue tracking and project management features, such as kanban boards, sprint planning, and milestone tracking. These features help teams organize and prioritize work, track progress, and communicate effectively, fostering a more transparent and efficient development process. In addition to these standard settings, some platforms offer advanced customization options for tailoring the project environment to specific requirements. For example, in GitHub, developers can create custom workflows using GitHub Actions, defining custom automation tasks and triggers to suit their unique development workflows. Similarly, in GitLab, developers can configure custom CI/CD pipelines using GitLab CI/CD configuration files, enabling advanced build and deployment scenarios. By taking advantage of these advanced customization options, developers can optimize their project settings to maximize productivity and efficiency. Overall, configuring project settings is a crucial step in setting up a successful development environment, enabling teams to customize their workflow, collaborate effectively, and deliver high-quality software efficiently. Whether adjusting visibility settings, configuring access controls, or integrating third-party services, mastering project settings is essential for navigating the complexities of modern software development workflows. In summary, project settings provide developers with the flexibility and control they need to tailor their development environment to their specific requirements and preferences, empowering them to collaborate effectively and deliver value to their users.

Chapter 4: Building and Managing Pipelines

In the realm of software development and continuous integration and continuous deployment (CI/CD), pipelines serve as the backbone of automated workflows, orchestrating the build, test, and deployment processes seamlessly. At their core, pipelines consist of various components that work together to automate the software delivery process, enabling teams to deliver code changes reliably and efficiently. One of the key components of a pipeline is the source control trigger, which initiates the pipeline whenever changes are pushed to the source code repository. This trigger mechanism ensures that the pipeline is executed automatically whenever new code changes are introduced, reducing manual intervention and enabling rapid feedback loops. In addition to the trigger mechanism, pipelines typically consist of stages, which represent distinct phases of the software delivery process. Each stage in the pipeline performs specific tasks, such as building the application, running tests, and deploying the application to production. By breaking down the software delivery process into stages, pipelines enable teams to modularize their workflows, making it easier to understand, debug, and maintain. Within each stage, pipelines often include one or more jobs, which represent individual units of work that need to be executed sequentially or in parallel. Jobs define the tasks that need to be performed, such as compiling code, running tests, or deploying artifacts, and provide the necessary configuration for executing those tasks. By defining jobs within stages, pipelines can parallelize workloads, optimizing resource utilization and reducing overall build times. Furthermore, pipelines can leverage various types of runners or agents to execute jobs, such as virtual machines, containers, or dedicated build servers. These runners provide the execution environment for jobs, ensuring that they are executed in a controlled and isolated environment. By using runners, pipelines can scale horizontally, accommodating the needs of growing development teams and complex software projects. Another essential component of pipelines is the artifact storage, which serves as a repository for build artifacts and other files generated during the pipeline execution. Artifacts can include compiled binaries, test reports, deployment packages, and configuration files, among others. By storing artifacts centrally, pipelines enable traceability and reproducibility, allowing teams to access and share build artifacts across different stages of the pipeline. Additionally, pipelines often incorporate built-in or custom tasks, which represent individual actions that need to be performed as part of the pipeline execution. Tasks can include actions such as copying files, running scripts, invoking external APIs, or interacting with cloud services. By defining tasks as part of the pipeline configuration, teams can automate repetitive tasks, standardize workflows, and ensure consistency across environments. Finally, pipelines typically include built-in logging and reporting mechanisms, which provide visibility into the pipeline execution and help diagnose issues or failures. Logging and reporting tools capture information such as job output, error messages, execution times, and resource utilization, enabling teams to monitor pipeline performance and troubleshoot issues effectively. By leveraging these components, pipelines serve as a powerful tool for automating the software delivery process, enabling teams to accelerate the pace of development, improve code quality, and deliver value to customers more efficiently. Whether building simple CI pipelines or complex CD pipelines, understanding the components of pipelines is essential for designing, implementing, and optimizing automated workflows effectively. In summary, pipelines represent the backbone of modern software development practices, providing the infrastructure for automating the build, test, and deployment processes. By understanding the components of pipelines and how they work together, teams can *streamline their development workflows, increase productivity, and deliver high-quality software with confidence.*

In the realm of continuous integration and continuous deployment (CI/CD), pipeline configuration plays a crucial role in determining the efficiency, reliability, and maintainability of automated workflows. As pipelines serve as the backbone of automated software delivery processes, it is essential to adhere to best practices when configuring pipelines to ensure optimal performance and effectiveness. One of the fundamental best practices in pipeline configuration is to keep pipelines simple and focused on specific tasks or stages of the software delivery process. By breaking down pipelines into smaller, more manageable components, teams can reduce complexity, improve visibility, and make it easier to debug and maintain pipelines over time. Another important best practice is to leverage version control for pipeline configuration files, storing them alongside the project source code in the same repository. By treating pipeline configuration as code, teams can track changes, collaborate more effectively, and ensure that pipeline configurations are consistent and reproducible across different environments. Additionally, version-controlled pipeline configuration files enable teams to roll back changes, audit modifications, and implement code review processes, further enhancing the quality and reliability of pipelines. When configuring pipelines, it is essential to adopt a modular approach, where reusable components and templates are used to standardize workflows and promote consistency across projects. By defining common patterns and templates for tasks such as building, testing, and deploying applications, teams can streamline pipeline configuration, reduce duplication, and improve maintainability. Furthermore, modular pipeline configurations make it easier to scale pipelines across different projects and teams, facilitating consistency and standardization in large and complex software development environments. Another best practice in pipeline configuration is to parameterize pipeline settings and variables, allowing for flexibility and customization across different environments and scenarios. By defining parameters for settings such as deployment targets, environment variables, and credentials, teams can create more versatile and adaptable pipelines that can be reused across different contexts. Parameterization also enhances security by minimizing the exposure of sensitive information in pipeline configuration files, reducing the risk of unauthorized access or data breaches. It is also essential to incorporate error handling and retry mechanisms into pipeline configurations, ensuring that pipelines can recover gracefully from failures and transient errors. By implementing strategies such as automatic retries, error notifications, and rollback procedures, teams can minimize downtime, mitigate risks, and maintain service availability during pipeline execution. Additionally, logging and monitoring play a crucial role in pipeline configuration, providing visibility into pipeline execution, performance, and outcomes. By capturing and analyzing pipeline logs, teams can identify bottlenecks, diagnose issues, and optimize pipeline performance over time. Integrating logging and monitoring tools into pipeline configurations enables teams to proactively monitor pipeline health, detect anomalies, and respond to incidents promptly. Security is another critical consideration when configuring pipelines, particularly when dealing with sensitive information such as credentials, access tokens, and deployment keys. Teams should implement robust security practices, such as encrypting sensitive data, restricting access to pipelines and resources, and regularly auditing pipeline configurations for vulnerabilities and compliance with security policies. Finally, it is essential to establish and enforce governance policies and standards for pipeline configuration, ensuring that pipelines adhere to organizational guidelines, best practices, and regulatory requirements. By implementing governance frameworks, teams can promote consistency, *compliance, and accountability in pipeline configuration, reducing the risk of errors, misconfigurations, and security breaches. In summary, pipeline configuration best practices encompass a range of strategies and principles aimed at optimizing the design, implementation, and management of automated software delivery pipelines. By adhering to these best practices, teams can create more efficient, reliable, and secure pipelines that enable them to deliver high-quality software with confidence and agility.*

Chapter 5: Implementing Continuous Integration

Setting up continuous integration (CI) pipelines is a critical step in modern software development workflows, enabling teams to automate the build, test, and validation processes for their applications. To begin setting up a CI pipeline, developers typically start by defining the pipeline configuration, which specifies the steps and tasks that need to be executed during the build and test process. One popular tool for defining CI pipelines is Jenkins, an open-source automation server that offers robust support for building, testing, and deploying applications. To create a new CI pipeline in Jenkins, developers can navigate to the Jenkins dashboard and select the option to create a new pipeline project. From there, developers can specify the pipeline configuration using a Jenkinsfile, which is a text file that defines the pipeline stages, steps, and dependencies. Within the Jenkinsfile, developers can define stages for tasks such as checking out the source code, compiling the application, running tests, and packaging artifacts for deployment. Additionally, developers can define steps within each stage, specifying the commands or scripts that need to be executed to perform specific tasks. For example, to compile a Java application, developers can use the javac command within a shell script step to compile source code files into bytecode. Similarly, to run unit tests for the application, developers can use the java -jar command to execute test cases using a testing framework such as JUnit. By defining these steps within the pipeline configuration, developers can automate the build and test process, ensuring that changes to the codebase are validated and verified automatically. Once the pipeline configuration is defined, developers can save the Jenkinsfile and trigger the pipeline to run by committing changes to the source code repository. Jenkins will automatically detect the changes and execute the pipeline according to the defined configuration, displaying the progress and results in the Jenkins dashboard. As the pipeline runs, developers can monitor the build status, view test results, and troubleshoot any issues that arise during the process. In addition to Jenkins, other CI/CD platforms such as GitLab CI, GitHub Actions, and Azure Pipelines offer similar capabilities for defining and executing CI pipelines. While the specific syntax and features may vary between platforms, the underlying principles of defining pipeline configurations and automating build and test processes remain consistent. In GitLab CI, for example, developers can define CI pipelines using a .gitlab-ci.yml file, which specifies the stages, jobs, and commands needed to build, test, and deploy applications. Similarly, in GitHub Actions, developers can define workflows using YAML syntax, specifying the steps and actions that need to be executed as part of the CI process. By leveraging these CI/CD platforms and tools, teams can streamline their development workflows, improve code quality, and accelerate the delivery of software applications. Additionally, CI pipelines enable teams to adopt practices such as continuous integration, where changes are integrated into the main codebase frequently, reducing integration issues and enabling faster feedback loops. Overall, setting up CI pipelines is a foundational step in modern software development practices, enabling teams to automate repetitive tasks, improve collaboration, and deliver high-quality software with confidence and efficiency.

Automated testing is a crucial aspect of continuous integration (CI) pipelines, enabling teams to validate code changes quickly and reliably as part of the software delivery process. By integrating automated tests into CI pipelines, teams can detect and address issues early in the development lifecycle, reducing the risk of introducing defects and improving overall code quality. One of the key benefits of automated testing in CI pipelines is the ability to execute tests automatically whenever changes are made to the codebase. This ensures that changes are validated promptly, providing rapid feedback to developers and enabling them to identify and fix issues before they escalate. To incorporate automated testing into CI pipelines, developers typically define test suites or test cases that cover different aspects of the application's functionality, including unit tests, integration tests, and end-to-end tests. Unit tests focus on validating individual components or units of code in isolation, ensuring that each component behaves as expected independently of other parts of the system. Integration tests, on the other hand, validate interactions between different components or modules of the application, verifying that they work together correctly as a whole. End-to-end tests validate the application's behavior from the user's perspective, simulating real-world scenarios and interactions to ensure that the application functions as intended in production environments. To execute automated tests in CI pipelines, developers can leverage testing frameworks and tools that support automation, such as JUnit, TestNG, Selenium, and Cypress. These frameworks provide APIs and utilities for writing and running tests programmatically, enabling developers to automate the execution of test cases as part of the CI process. For example, to run unit tests written in Java using JUnit, developers can use the mvn test command with Maven, a popular build automation tool for Java projects. Similarly, to run end-to-end tests written in JavaScript using Cypress, developers can use the *cypress run command in a CI pipeline to execute test cases against a web application. By incorporating these commands into CI pipeline configurations, developers can automate the execution of tests and integrate them seamlessly into the software delivery process. In addition to executing tests, CI pipelines also generate test reports and artifacts that provide visibility into test results and outcomes. These reports include information such as test pass/fail status, code coverage metrics, and performance statistics, enabling teams to assess the quality and stability of the codebase. By analyzing test reports, teams can identify areas for improvement, prioritize bug fixes, and track progress over time, fostering a culture of continuous improvement and quality assurance. Furthermore, CI pipelines can be configured to enforce quality gates and thresholds based on test results, preventing code changes from being merged if they fail to meet predefined criteria. For example, teams can set up CI pipelines to fail automatically if code changes result in a decrease in test coverage or if critical tests fail, ensuring that only high-quality, reliable code is integrated into the main codebase. By enforcing quality gates, teams can maintain code stability, reduce technical debt, and uphold standards for code quality and reliability. In summary, automated testing in CI pipelines is a powerful practice for improving code quality, accelerating development cycles, and reducing risks in software projects. By incorporating automated tests into CI pipelines, teams can validate code changes continuously, detect issues early, and deliver high-quality software with confidence and efficiency.*

Chapter 6: Deploying Applications with Azure DevOps

Setting up a continuous deployment (CD) pipeline is a crucial step in modern software development workflows, enabling teams to automate the deployment of code changes to production environments quickly and reliably. Unlike continuous integration (CI) pipelines, which focus on building and testing code changes, CD pipelines extend the automation process to include deployment tasks, such as packaging artifacts, provisioning infrastructure, and deploying applications. To begin setting up a CD pipeline, developers typically start by defining the pipeline configuration, which specifies the steps and tasks that need to be executed during the deployment process. Similar to CI pipelines, CD pipelines can be defined using configuration files or scripts that describe the deployment workflow, dependencies, and deployment targets. One popular tool for defining CD pipelines is Jenkins, which offers robust support for automating deployment tasks and integrating with various deployment targets, such as cloud platforms, container registries, and deployment tools. To create a new CD pipeline in Jenkins, developers can use the Jenkins pipeline syntax to define stages, steps, and dependencies for deploying applications. Within the pipeline configuration, developers can specify tasks such as packaging application artifacts, configuring deployment environments, and executing deployment scripts. For example, to deploy a web application to a Kubernetes cluster, developers can use the kubectl command within a shell script step to apply Kubernetes manifests and deploy the application containers. Similarly, to deploy a serverless application to AWS Lambda, developers can use the AWS CLI commands within a script step to package and deploy the application code to Lambda functions. By defining these deployment tasks within the pipeline configuration, developers can automate the deployment process and ensure that changes are deployed consistently and reliably across different environments. In addition to Jenkins, other CD tools and platforms such as GitLab CI, GitHub Actions, and Azure Pipelines offer similar capabilities for defining and executing CD pipelines. While the specific syntax and features may vary between platforms, the underlying principles of automating deployment tasks and orchestrating deployment workflows remain consistent. In GitLab CI, for example, developers can define CD pipelines using a .gitlab-ci.yml file, which specifies the stages, jobs, and commands needed to deploy applications. Similarly, in GitHub Actions, developers can define deployment workflows using YAML syntax, specifying the steps and actions that need to be executed as part of the deployment process. By leveraging these CD platforms and tools, teams can streamline their deployment workflows, improve deployment frequency, and reduce the time-to-market for software applications. Additionally, CD pipelines enable teams to adopt practices such as continuous deployment, where changes are automatically deployed to production environments after passing automated tests and quality checks. This approach enables teams to deliver new features and updates to users quickly, reducing manual intervention and accelerating time-to-value. In addition to automating deployment tasks, CD pipelines also provide visibility into the deployment process, enabling teams to monitor deployment progress, track deployment history, and troubleshoot deployment issues effectively. By capturing and analyzing deployment logs and metrics, teams can identify bottlenecks, diagnose issues, and optimize deployment performance over time. Integrating logging and monitoring tools into CD pipelines enables teams to proactively monitor deployment health, detect anomalies, and respond to incidents promptly. Security is another critical consideration when setting up CD pipelines, particularly when deploying applications to production environments. Teams should implement *robust security practices, such as encrypting sensitive data, restricting access to deployment targets, and regularly auditing pipeline configurations for vulnerabilities and compliance with security policies. By implementing security controls, teams can reduce the risk of unauthorized access, data breaches, and compliance violations in their CD pipelines. Finally, it is essential to establish and enforce governance policies and standards for CD pipeline setup, ensuring that pipelines adhere to organizational guidelines, best practices, and regulatory requirements. By implementing governance frameworks, teams can promote consistency, compliance, and accountability in CD pipeline setup, reducing the risk of errors, misconfigurations, and security breaches. In summary, setting up CD pipelines is a foundational step in modern software development practices, enabling teams to automate deployment tasks, improve deployment frequency, and accelerate time-to-market for software applications. By adhering to best practices and leveraging CD platforms and tools, teams can streamline their deployment workflows, increase productivity, and deliver high-quality software with confidence and efficiency.*

Deployment strategies are essential components of modern software development processes, determining how changes are released and made available to users in production environments. One of the most common deployment strategies is the blue-green deployment, which involves maintaining two identical production environments: one active (blue) and one inactive (green). With this strategy, new changes are deployed to the inactive environment (green), allowing teams to test and validate them thoroughly before switching traffic from the active environment (blue) to the updated one (green). This approach minimizes downtime and risk, as the switch between environments can be performed seamlessly with minimal disruption to users. To implement a blue-green deployment, developers can use deployment automation tools such as Kubernetes or AWS Elastic Beanstalk, which provide built-in support for blue-green deployments. For example, in Kubernetes, developers can define two deployment objects representing the blue and green environments, each with its own set of pods, services, and configurations. By updating the deployment objects with the new changes and gradually shifting traffic from one environment to the other, teams can perform blue-green deployments safely and efficiently. Another popular deployment strategy is canary deployment, which involves releasing changes to a small subset of users or servers initially before gradually rolling them out to the entire user base. With canary deployments, teams can monitor the performance and stability of *the changes in real-time, allowing them to detect and mitigate issues before fully deploying the changes to all users. To implement a canary deployment, developers can use deployment automation tools such as Spinnaker or Istio, which offer built-in support for canary deployments. For example, in Spinnaker, developers can define a canary deployment pipeline that deploys changes to a small percentage of servers or clusters, monitors key metrics such as latency and error rates, and automatically promotes the changes to the rest of the infrastructure if they meet predefined criteria. Additionally, some deployment strategies focus on minimizing downtime and disruption during the deployment process, such as rolling deployments and blue-green deployments. With rolling deployments, changes are gradually rolled out to servers or clusters one at a time, allowing the application to remain available throughout the deployment process. This approach ensures that users experience minimal disruption and downtime, as only a small portion of the infrastructure is affected at any given time. To implement a rolling deployment, developers can use deployment automation tools such as Kubernetes or AWS CodeDeploy, which provide built-in support for rolling deployments. For example, in Kubernetes, developers can update the deployment objects with the new changes, and Kubernetes will automatically* roll out the changes to pods in a controlled manner, ensuring that the application remains available and responsive during the deployment process. In addition to these deployment strategies, teams can also leverage feature flags and toggles to control the visibility and behavior of new features and changes in production environments. By using feature flags, teams can release changes to production environments gradually, allowing them to monitor and evaluate the impact of the changes on user experience and performance before fully enabling them for all users. To implement feature flags, developers can use feature flagging tools and libraries such as LaunchDarkly or Rollout, which provide APIs and SDKs for integrating feature flags into applications and controlling their behavior dynamically. By incorporating feature flags into their deployment strategies, teams can release changes with confidence, knowing that they can easily roll back or adjust features based on user feedback and performance metrics. Overall, deployment strategies play a crucial role in the success of software development projects, enabling teams to release changes safely, efficiently, and with minimal disruption to users. By adopting best practices and leveraging deployment automation tools and techniques, teams can streamline their deployment workflows, improve code quality, and deliver value to users more rapidly and reliably.

Chapter 7: Monitoring and Logging in Azure DevOps

Monitoring tools integration is a fundamental aspect of modern software development and operations, facilitating real-time visibility into the health, performance, and availability of applications and infrastructure. These tools provide insights and metrics that help teams identify and diagnose issues, optimize performance, and ensure the reliability of their systems. One of the key benefits of monitoring tools integration is the ability to detect and respond to issues proactively before they impact users or business operations. By monitoring key metrics such as CPU utilization, memory usage, and response times, teams can identify trends, anomalies, and performance bottlenecks early, allowing them to take corrective actions promptly. To integrate monitoring tools into software applications and infrastructure, teams can leverage a variety of techniques and approaches. One common approach is to instrument applications with monitoring agents or libraries that capture and report metrics to monitoring platforms. For example, in Java applications, developers can use libraries such as Micrometer or Dropwizard Metrics to collect and expose application metrics, which can then be ingested by monitoring platforms such as Prometheus or Datadog. Similarly, in containerized environments, teams can use tools like Prometheus or Telegraf to scrape metrics from containers and orchestration platforms such as Kubernetes or Docker Swarm, providing visibility into resource usage, performance, and application health. Another approach to monitoring tools integration is to leverage built-in monitoring capabilities offered by cloud providers and platforms. For example, cloud providers such as AWS, Azure, and Google Cloud offer native monitoring services that provide insights into infrastructure metrics, application performance, and service health. By integrating these services into their environments, teams can gain visibility into the performance and availability of their cloud resources and applications, enabling them to monitor, troubleshoot, and optimize their deployments effectively. Additionally, teams can use configuration management tools such as Ansible, Puppet, or Chef to automate the deployment and configuration of monitoring agents and tools across their infrastructure. By defining monitoring configurations as code, teams can ensure consistency, repeatability, and scalability in their monitoring setups, reducing manual effort and minimizing the risk of misconfigurations. For example, teams can use Ansible playbooks to install and configure monitoring agents on servers, define alerting thresholds and policies, and integrate monitoring dashboards with collaboration tools such as Slack or Microsoft Teams. By automating these tasks, teams can streamline their monitoring setup and maintenance processes, enabling them to focus on delivering value to users and customers. In addition to collecting metrics and monitoring infrastructure, teams can also use logging and tracing tools to capture and analyze application logs and traces. Logging tools such as Elasticsearch, Logstash, and Kibana (ELK Stack) or centralized logging services like AWS CloudWatch Logs and Azure Monitor Logs enable teams to aggregate, search, and visualize log data from distributed systems and applications. Similarly, tracing tools such as Jaeger, Zipkin, or AWS X-Ray provide distributed tracing capabilities, allowing teams to trace requests across microservices and identify latency bottlenecks and performance issues. By integrating logging and tracing tools into their monitoring setups, teams can gain deeper insights into application behavior, troubleshoot issues more effectively, and optimize performance and reliability. Another important aspect of monitoring tools integration is alerting and notification management. Monitoring platforms typically offer alerting features that allow teams to define alert rules and thresholds based on predefined metrics and conditions. When an alert is triggered, teams *can configure notification channels such as email, SMS, or chat applications to notify stakeholders and responders promptly. By configuring alerting and notification channels, teams can ensure timely responses to incidents and minimize the impact of downtime or service disruptions on users and business operations. Overall, monitoring tools integration is essential for maintaining the health, performance, and reliability of modern software applications and infrastructure. By leveraging monitoring tools and techniques, teams can gain visibility into their systems, detect and respond to issues proactively, and optimize performance and reliability effectively. Whether monitoring on-premises infrastructure, cloud environments, or microservices architectures, integrating monitoring tools into development and operations workflows is critical for delivering high-quality software and services to users and customers. Logging is a critical aspect of software development and operations, providing visibility into the behavior, performance, and health of applications and systems. Effective logging practices enable teams to monitor, troubleshoot, and optimize their applications, identify issues quickly, and ensure reliability and availability. One of the key principles of logging best practices is to log relevant and actionable information that helps diagnose issues and understand system behavior. Logs should* capture important events, errors, warnings, and performance metrics, providing insights into the execution flow and runtime characteristics of applications. To implement logging best practices, developers can use logging frameworks and libraries that support structured logging and log levels. Structured logging allows developers to log events with key-value pairs, making it easier to search, filter, and analyze log data effectively. Log levels such as DEBUG, INFO, WARN, ERROR, and FATAL provide granularity in logging, allowing developers to control the verbosity of log messages and prioritize critical events. For example, in Java applications, developers can use the SLF4J logging facade with a logging implementation such as Logback or Log4j to configure log levels and format log messages according to their requirements. By configuring log levels appropriately, teams can strike a balance between capturing relevant information and minimizing log volume, ensuring that logs remain useful and manageable. Another best practice in logging is to log contextual information along with log messages, such as request identifiers, user IDs, timestamps, and execution context. Contextual information helps correlate log messages to specific requests or transactions, making it easier to trace the flow of execution and troubleshoot issues effectively. To log contextual information, developers can use log *appenders and enrichers provided by logging frameworks, or they can use built-in features of logging libraries to inject context into log messages dynamically. For example, in Node.js applications, developers can use middleware functions such as morgan or winston-express to log HTTP request and response details, including headers, status codes, and request URLs. By logging contextual information, teams can gain insights into application behavior, detect patterns, and diagnose issues more accurately. Additionally, logging best practices emphasize the importance of log aggregation and centralization, where logs from multiple sources are collected, aggregated, and stored in a centralized location for analysis and monitoring. Centralized logging platforms such as Elasticsearch, Logstash, and Kibana (ELK Stack) or cloud-based logging services like AWS CloudWatch Logs and Azure Monitor Logs provide capabilities for collecting, indexing, and analyzing log data at scale. By centralizing logs, teams can gain visibility into the entire system, correlate events across different components, and identify trends and anomalies effectively. To centralize logs, teams can use logging agents or libraries that forward log messages to a centralized logging platform over a network connection. For example, in Docker containers, developers can configure the Docker logging driver to forward container logs to a centralized logging* endpoint such as the ELK Stack or a cloud-based logging service. By centralizing logs, teams can simplify log management, reduce storage costs, and improve log search and analysis capabilities. Security is another important consideration in logging best practices, particularly when logging sensitive information such as user credentials, personal data, or payment information. Teams should implement encryption and access controls to protect sensitive log data from unauthorized access or disclosure. Additionally, teams should configure log rotation and retention policies to manage log storage effectively, ensuring that log data is retained for the appropriate duration and deleted securely when no longer needed. By implementing security controls and policies, teams can mitigate the risk of data breaches and compliance violations associated with logging sensitive information. In summary, logging best practices play a crucial role in software development and operations, enabling teams to monitor, troubleshoot, and optimize their applications effectively. By following best practices such as logging relevant and actionable information, logging contextual information, centralizing logs, and implementing security controls, teams can create robust logging solutions that provide visibility, reliability, and security across their applications and systems. Whether logging in monolithic applications, microservices architectures, *or cloud environments, adopting logging best practices is essential for delivering high-quality software and services to users and customers.*

Chapter 8: Collaboration and Communication Tools in Azure DevOps

Utilizing Azure Boards is an essential aspect of managing and tracking software development projects effectively within the Azure DevOps ecosystem. Azure Boards provides a robust set of tools and features designed to facilitate collaboration, planning, and tracking of work items across teams and projects. One of the key features of Azure Boards is the ability to create and manage work items, which represent tasks, user stories, bugs, or other units of work within a project. Work items can be customized to capture specific details such as priority, status, assignee, and effort estimates, providing teams with the flexibility to track and manage work items according to their requirements. To create a work item in Azure Boards, users can navigate to the Boards module within the Azure DevOps portal and select the option to create a new work item. From there, users can choose the type of work item they want to create, such as a user story or a bug, and fill in the relevant details, including title, description, and assignee. Additionally, users can add tags, attachments, and custom fields to work items to provide additional context and information. By creating work items in Azure Boards, teams can capture requirements, track progress, and prioritize tasks effectively, enabling them to deliver value to users and stakeholders more efficiently. Another key feature of Azure Boards is the ability to plan and manage work using Agile methodologies such as Scrum or Kanban. Azure Boards provides customizable Agile boards that allow teams to visualize and track the flow of work through different stages of development, from backlog grooming to deployment. Agile boards can be configured to show work items in different states, such as new, in progress, or done, allowing teams to track progress and identify bottlenecks easily. Additionally, Agile boards support features such as swimlanes, sprint planning, and burndown charts, providing teams with the tools they need to plan and execute Agile projects effectively. To configure an Agile board in Azure Boards, users can navigate to the Boards module and create a new board using the Agile template. From there, users can customize the board layout, add columns and swimlanes, and configure settings such as team capacity and sprint duration. By configuring Agile boards in Azure Boards, teams can align on priorities, track progress, and adapt to changing requirements more effectively, enabling them to deliver value iteratively and incrementally. In addition to Agile boards, Azure Boards also supports advanced planning and *tracking features such as backlogs, sprint planning, and release management. Backlogs allow teams to prioritize and manage work items at the project level, providing a centralized view of all planned work. Sprint planning enables teams to plan and commit to work for upcoming sprints, defining sprint goals, and estimating effort for individual tasks. Release management features allow teams to plan and coordinate releases, defining release milestones, tracking progress, and managing dependencies. By leveraging these planning and tracking features in Azure Boards, teams can coordinate and execute complex projects more effectively, ensuring that work is delivered on time and within budget. Additionally, Azure Boards integrates seamlessly with other Azure DevOps services such as Azure Repos, Azure Pipelines, and Azure Test Plans, providing teams with end-to-end visibility and traceability across the software development lifecycle. Work items created in Azure Boards can be linked to source code changes, build artifacts, and test results, enabling teams to trace requirements to implementation and ensure that quality is maintained throughout the development process. By integrating Azure Boards with other Azure DevOps services, teams can streamline their workflows, improve collaboration, and deliver high-quality software more efficiently. Overall, utilizing Azure Boards is essential for managing and tracking software development projects effectively within the Azure DevOps ecosystem. By leveraging features such as work item management, Agile boards, and advanced planning and tracking capabilities, teams can collaborate, plan, and execute projects more efficiently, enabling them to deliver value to users and stakeholders with confidence and agility. Integrating with Microsoft Teams offers teams a seamless collaboration experience by bringing together communication, collaboration, and productivity tools in one platform. Microsoft Teams serves as a central hub for team communication, enabling users to chat, meet, call, and collaborate on documents and projects in real-time. One of the key benefits of integrating Azure DevOps with Microsoft Teams is the ability to receive notifications and updates directly within Teams channels, keeping team members informed and engaged with project activities. To integrate Azure DevOps with Microsoft Teams, teams can leverage the Azure Boards app for Teams, which provides a set of connectors and bots that enable bidirectional communication between Azure DevOps and Teams. By installing the Azure Boards app in Teams, teams can configure notifications for specific events such as work item updates, pull request approvals, or build completions, ensuring that relevant information is shared with team members in real-time. Additionally, teams can use the Azure*

Pipelines app for Teams to monitor build and release pipelines, track progress, and receive alerts on pipeline failures or regressions. To install the Azure Boards app for Teams, users can navigate to the Teams app store, search for "Azure Boards," and install the app into their Teams workspace. Once installed, users can configure connectors and subscriptions to receive notifications for specific events from Azure DevOps. For example, to receive notifications for work item updates, users can configure a connector that sends messages to a Teams channel whenever a work item is assigned to them or when its status changes. By configuring connectors and subscriptions, teams can customize their notification experience in Teams, ensuring that they receive timely updates on project activities and milestones. In addition to notifications, teams can also use bots and commands in Teams to interact with Azure DevOps directly from the Teams interface. For example, teams can use the Azure Boards bot to create new work items, update work item details, or query work item status without leaving the Teams app. Similarly, teams can use the Azure Pipelines bot to trigger pipeline runs, view build and release statuses, and approve deployments, all within the Teams interface. By leveraging bots and commands in Teams, teams can streamline their workflows, reduce context switching, and collaborate more effectively on *projects. Another benefit of integrating Azure DevOps with Microsoft Teams is the ability to embed Azure DevOps artifacts and dashboards directly within Teams channels and tabs. Teams can create custom tabs in Teams channels that display Azure DevOps dashboards, boards, queries, or specific work items, providing team members with instant access to project information and insights. To add Azure DevOps artifacts to Teams tabs, users can use the Azure DevOps app for Teams, which provides a set of pre-built tabs and widgets that can be added to Teams channels. For example, teams can add a "Sprint Overview" tab to their Teams channel that displays a dashboard widget showing sprint progress, burndown charts, and work item statistics from Azure DevOps. By embedding Azure DevOps artifacts in Teams tabs, teams can centralize project information, foster transparency, and improve collaboration within their Teams channels. Additionally, integrating Azure DevOps with Microsoft Teams enables teams to leverage the rich ecosystem of apps and integrations available in Teams to extend and customize their collaboration experience further. Teams can integrate with third-party services such as Jira, GitHub, or Slack, allowing them to consolidate project activities and communications within the Teams interface. For example, teams can use the GitHub app for Teams to receive notifications for code reviews, pull* requests, and issue updates directly within Teams channels, enabling seamless collaboration between development teams using different tools. By integrating with third-party services and apps, teams can tailor their collaboration experience in Teams to their specific needs and preferences, enhancing productivity and efficiency. In summary, integrating Azure DevOps with Microsoft Teams offers teams a powerful collaboration platform that combines communication, collaboration, and productivity tools in one interface. By leveraging connectors, bots, tabs, and integrations, teams can streamline their workflows, stay informed about project activities, and collaborate more effectively on projects, ultimately driving better outcomes and delivering value to users and stakeholders.

Chapter 9: Managing Work Items and Boards

Work item tracking is a fundamental aspect of software development and project management, enabling teams to manage and track tasks, issues, and requirements throughout the software development lifecycle. In modern software development practices, work item tracking is typically managed using specialized tools and platforms such as Azure DevOps, which provide features and capabilities designed to streamline the tracking and management of work items. One of the key benefits of work item tracking is the ability to capture and prioritize tasks and requirements effectively, ensuring that teams stay focused on delivering value to users and stakeholders. Work items can represent various types of work, including user stories, bugs, tasks, features, and epics, each with its own set of attributes and properties. For example, a user story work item may include fields such as title, description, acceptance criteria, priority, and effort estimate, while a bug work item may include fields such as steps to reproduce, severity, and resolution status. By capturing detailed information in work items, teams can communicate expectations, clarify requirements, and ensure alignment on project goals and deliverables. To create a work item in Azure DevOps, users can navigate to the Boards module within the Azure DevOps portal and select the option to create a new work item. From there, users can choose the type of work item they want to create, such as a user story or a bug, and fill in the relevant details, including title, description, and assigned team member. Additionally, users can add tags, attachments, and custom fields to work items to provide additional context and information. By creating work items in Azure DevOps, teams can capture requirements, track progress, and prioritize tasks effectively, enabling them to deliver value to users and stakeholders more efficiently. One of the key features of work item tracking in Azure DevOps is the ability to organize and manage work items using Agile methodologies such as Scrum or Kanban. Azure DevOps provides customizable Agile boards that allow teams to visualize and track the flow of work through different stages of development, from backlog grooming to deployment. Agile boards can be configured to show work items in different states, such as new, in progress, or done, allowing teams to track progress and identify bottlenecks easily. Additionally, Agile boards support features such as swimlanes, sprint planning, and burndown charts, providing teams with the tools they need to plan and execute Agile projects effectively. To configure an Agile board in Azure DevOps, users can navigate to the Boards module and create a new board using the Agile template. From there, users can customize the board layout, add columns and swimlanes, and configure settings such as team capacity and sprint duration. By configuring Agile boards in Azure DevOps, teams can align on priorities, track progress, and adapt to changing requirements more effectively, enabling them to deliver value iteratively and incrementally. In addition to Agile boards, Azure DevOps also supports advanced planning and tracking features such as backlogs, sprint planning, and release management. Backlogs allow teams to prioritize and manage work items at the project level, providing a centralized view of all planned work. Sprint planning enables teams to plan and commit to work for upcoming sprints, defining sprint goals, and estimating effort for individual tasks. Release management features allow teams to plan and coordinate releases, defining release milestones, tracking progress, and managing dependencies. By leveraging these planning and tracking features in Azure DevOps, teams can coordinate and execute complex projects more effectively, ensuring that work is delivered on time and within budget. Overall, work item tracking is a critical aspect of software development and project management, enabling teams to manage and track tasks, issues, and requirements effectively throughout the software development lifecycle. By *leveraging tools and platforms such as Azure DevOps, teams can capture requirements, prioritize tasks, and track progress more efficiently, enabling them to deliver value to users and stakeholders with confidence and agility.*

Agile planning techniques are essential for teams to effectively plan and manage their work in iterative and incremental software development projects. Agile methodologies such as Scrum and Kanban emphasize flexibility, collaboration, and continuous improvement, enabling teams to respond to changing requirements and deliver value to users more efficiently. One of the key principles of Agile planning is prioritization, where teams focus on delivering the most valuable features and functionalities to users first. Prioritization is typically done using techniques such as user story mapping, MoSCoW prioritization, or value-based prioritization, where features are ranked based on their business value, complexity, and dependencies. User story mapping involves breaking down features into user stories and organizing them into a visual map that represents the user journey, helping teams identify the most critical paths and prioritize work accordingly. MoSCoW prioritization categorizes features into Must-have, Should-have, Could-have, and Won't-have categories, allowing teams to focus on delivering the most critical features first while deferring less essential ones. Value-based prioritization involves assessing features based on their potential impact on users and the business, prioritizing those that provide the highest value or return on investment. By prioritizing work effectively, teams can maximize the value delivered to users and stakeholders with limited time and resources. Sprint planning is another essential Agile planning technique that involves defining the scope and goals for a sprint, typically lasting one to four weeks. During sprint planning, teams select a set of user stories or tasks from the backlog and commit to delivering them by the end of the sprint. Sprint planning sessions typically include discussions about the objectives of the sprint, the estimated effort for each task, and any dependencies or risks that need to be addressed. To facilitate sprint planning, teams can use Agile planning tools such as Jira, Azure DevOps, or Trello, which provide features for managing backlogs, estimating effort, and tracking progress. For example, in Azure DevOps, teams can use the Sprint Planning Board to drag and drop user stories from the backlog into the sprint backlog, estimate effort using story points or hours, and track progress throughout the sprint. By conducting sprint planning sessions regularly, teams can ensure alignment on project goals, identify dependencies and risks early, and commit to delivering value incrementally. Another Agile planning technique is the use of timeboxing to limit the duration of meetings and activities, ensuring that teams stay focused and make progress efficiently. Timeboxing involves setting fixed time limits for meetings, discussions, or tasks, allowing teams to allocate time effectively and avoid overcommitting to work. For example, in Scrum, daily stand-up meetings are timeboxed to 15 minutes, where team members provide updates on their progress, discuss any obstacles, and plan their work for the day. By timeboxing activities, teams can foster collaboration, maintain momentum, and prevent meetings from becoming overly lengthy or unproductive. Iterative planning is another Agile planning technique that involves breaking down work into small, manageable increments and delivering them iteratively over time. Instead of trying to plan and execute all work upfront, teams focus on delivering a subset of features or functionalities in each iteration, incorporating feedback and learning from each cycle to inform future planning and execution. Iterative planning enables teams to adapt to changing requirements, mitigate risks, and deliver value incrementally, reducing the likelihood of project delays or failures. For example, in Kanban, teams use a continuous flow approach to plan and execute work, with tasks moving through different stages of the workflow as capacity allows. By continuously reprioritizing and *refining the backlog based on feedback and changing priorities, teams can ensure that they are delivering the most valuable work at any given time. Overall, Agile planning techniques play a crucial role in enabling teams to deliver value iteratively and incrementally in software development projects. By prioritizing work effectively, conducting regular sprint planning sessions, timeboxing activities, and embracing iterative planning, teams can adapt to changing requirements, mitigate risks, and deliver high-quality software more efficiently. Whether using Scrum, Kanban, or a combination of Agile methodologies, mastering Agile planning techniques is essential for success in today's fast-paced and dynamic software development landscape.*

Chapter 10: Exam Preparation and Practice Exercises

Understanding exam objectives is crucial for success in any certification or assessment, as it provides a roadmap for what candidates need to know and demonstrate proficiency in. Exam objectives typically outline the knowledge, skills, and competencies that candidates are expected to possess in order to pass the exam and earn the certification. These objectives are often based on industry best practices, standards, and guidelines, and are designed to ensure that certified professionals have the requisite knowledge and expertise to perform effectively in their roles. For example, in the context of the Azure DevOps Engineer certification exam (Exam AZ-400), the exam objectives cover a wide range of topics related to designing and implementing DevOps solutions using Microsoft Azure. These topics include but are not limited to, implementing DevOps development processes, implementing continuous integration, continuous delivery, and continuous deployment (CI/CD) pipelines, implementing dependency management, and integrating security, compliance, and identity management into DevOps processes. To prepare for the exam, candidates should thoroughly review the exam objectives and identify areas where they need to strengthen their knowledge and skills. This may involve studying relevant documentation, taking online courses or training, practicing with hands-on labs and exercises, and seeking guidance from experienced professionals or mentors. By focusing on the exam objectives, candidates can tailor their preparation efforts and ensure that they are adequately prepared to demonstrate proficiency in the areas covered by the exam. Additionally, understanding exam objectives can help candidates approach exam questions strategically and effectively. By knowing what topics are covered by the exam, candidates can prioritize their study efforts and allocate time and resources accordingly. For example, if a candidate knows that a significant portion of the exam will focus on CI/CD pipelines, they can dedicate more time to studying this topic and ensuring that they understand key concepts, best practices, and tools related to CI/CD. Furthermore, understanding exam objectives can help candidates identify gaps in their knowledge and skills and take steps to address them proactively. For example, if a candidate realizes that they are less familiar with certain aspects of Azure DevOps, such as integrating security or managing dependencies, they can focus on studying these areas in more depth and practicing with relevant tools and techniques. By identifying and addressing *knowledge gaps early in the preparation process, candidates can increase their chances of success on the exam and earn the certification. In addition to studying the exam objectives, candidates should also familiarize themselves with the format and structure of the exam. This may include understanding the types of questions that may be asked, the time limit for the exam, and any specific instructions or guidelines provided by the exam provider. By knowing what to expect on exam day, candidates can feel more confident and prepared, which can help alleviate test anxiety and improve performance. Finally, candidates should take advantage of practice exams and mock tests to assess their readiness for the exam and identify areas where they may need additional study or practice. Many exam providers offer practice exams or sample questions that mimic the format and difficulty level of the actual exam, allowing candidates to gauge their progress and identify areas for improvement. By taking practice exams and reviewing feedback, candidates can identify weaknesses, refine their study strategy, and increase their confidence going into the exam. Overall, understanding exam objectives is essential for success on any certification or assessment. By thoroughly reviewing the exam objectives, tailoring study efforts accordingly, familiarizing themselves with the exam format and structure, and utilizing practice exams, candidates can increase their chances of passing the exam and earning the certification. Whether preparing for the Azure DevOps Engineer certification exam or any other exam, a solid understanding of exam objectives is a critical first step towards achieving certification success.*

Practice exercises and mock tests are invaluable tools for candidates preparing for certification exams, providing an opportunity to reinforce learning, assess knowledge retention, and build confidence in exam-taking skills. These exercises and tests simulate the format, content, and difficulty level of the actual exam, allowing candidates to familiarize themselves with the types of questions they may encounter and the time constraints they will face. By completing practice exercises and mock tests, candidates can identify areas of strength and weakness, enabling them to focus their study efforts more effectively. For example, candidates may discover that they are particularly strong in certain topics, such as CI/CD pipelines or security concepts, but may need additional review in other areas, such as Azure services or DevOps best practices. Armed with this information, candidates can tailor their study plan to address their specific needs and prioritize topics accordingly. Practice exercises typically involve hands-on activities or scenarios that require candidates to apply their knowledge and skills in a real-world context. For example, candidates may be asked to configure a CI/CD pipeline using Azure DevOps, troubleshoot a deployment issue, or analyze log data to identify performance bottlenecks. These exercises not only reinforce theoretical concepts but also provide practical experience that is directly applicable to the job role. By engaging in hands-on practice, candidates can develop proficiency in using relevant tools and technologies, which is essential for success on the exam and in real-world scenarios. Mock tests, on the other hand, simulate the experience of taking the actual exam by presenting a series of exam-style questions under timed conditions. These tests are designed to assess candidates' knowledge, comprehension, and problem-solving abilities within the constraints of the exam format. Mock tests may cover a broad range of topics and question types, including multiple-choice, scenario-based, and interactive questions, similar to those found on the actual exam. By completing mock tests, candidates can gauge their readiness for the exam, identify areas where they may need additional study or practice, and familiarize themselves with the pace and rhythm of the exam. Mock tests also provide an opportunity for candidates to practice exam-taking strategies, such as managing time effectively, eliminating incorrect answer choices, and interpreting questions accurately. One common approach to preparing for certification exams is to use a combination of practice exercises and mock tests throughout the study period. Candidates may start by reviewing study materials and completing practice exercises to build foundational knowledge and skills. As they progress in their studies, candidates can then transition to mock tests to assess their readiness and identify areas for further review. By alternating between practice exercises and mock tests, candidates can reinforce learning, track progress, and build confidence over time. Many resources are available to help candidates access practice exercises and mock tests for certification exams. These may include official study guides and practice exams provided by exam vendors, as well as online training platforms, forums, and communities. Additionally, some certification programs offer practice labs or virtual environments where candidates can practice hands-on skills in a controlled setting. When using practice exercises and mock tests, it's essential for candidates to approach them with a growth mindset and a willingness to learn from mistakes. Even if a candidate does not perform well on a practice exercise or mock test initially, they can use the experience as an opportunity to identify areas for improvement and adjust their study strategy accordingly. By persisting and continuing to practice, candidates can gradually build confidence and proficiency in the topics covered by the exam, increasing their chances of success on exam day. Overall, practice exercises and mock tests are essential components of a comprehensive study plan for certification exams. By engaging in hands-on practice, simulating exam conditions, and identifying areas for improvement, candidates can prepare effectively, maximize their performance, and achieve their certification goals. Whether preparing for the Azure DevOps Engineer certification exam or any other certification, leveraging practice exercises and mock tests is key to success in demonstrating proficiency and earning recognition for one's skills and expertise.

BOOK 2
MASTERING CONTINUOUS INTEGRATION AND
CONTINUOUS DEPLOYMENT WITH AZURE DEVOPS:
EXAM AZ-400

ROB BOTWRIGHT

Chapter 1: Understanding Continuous Integration (CI) Principles

Continuous Integration (CI) is a critical practice in modern software development, facilitating collaboration, improving code quality, and accelerating the delivery of software products. At its core, CI is a development practice where developers integrate their code changes into a shared repository frequently, typically several times a day. The primary goal of CI is to detect and address integration errors early in the development process, reducing the risk of costly defects and ensuring that software remains in a releasable state at all times. By integrating code changes frequently, CI helps teams identify issues and conflicts sooner, allowing them to resolve them more efficiently and preventing them from accumulating over time. This iterative approach to integration fosters a culture of collaboration and transparency among team members, as everyone is responsible for ensuring the integrity and stability of the codebase. One of the key benefits of CI is its ability to automate the build and test process, enabling teams to validate changes quickly and reliably. When a developer commits code changes to the shared repository, CI servers automatically trigger a series of build and test jobs to verify the correctness and quality of the code. These jobs may include compiling code, running unit tests, performing code analysis, and deploying applications to test environments. By automating these repetitive and time-consuming tasks, CI frees up developers to focus on more valuable activities, such as writing code and implementing new features. Additionally, CI provides immediate feedback to developers about the quality of their code changes, helping them identify and address issues before they escalate. For example, if a build job fails due to a compilation error or a failing test, developers are notified immediately, allowing them to investigate and fix the issue promptly. This rapid feedback loop encourages developers to adopt best practices such as writing modular, testable code, and performing code reviews, leading to higher code quality and fewer defects. Another important benefit of CI is its role in enabling Continuous Delivery (CD) and Continuous Deployment (CD) practices. Continuous Delivery is a software development approach where code changes are automatically built, tested, and prepared for release, ready to be deployed to production at any time. Continuous Deployment takes this a step further by automating the deployment of code changes to production environments as soon as they pass all tests and checks. CI serves as the foundation for both

Continuous Delivery and Continuous Deployment, providing the necessary infrastructure and processes to ensure that code changes can be released safely and reliably. By adopting CI, teams can reduce the time and effort required to deliver software updates to users, enabling them to respond quickly to customer feedback and market demands. Additionally, CI helps teams mitigate the risk associated with deploying changes to production environments by catching integration errors and regressions early in the development process. This reduces the likelihood of costly downtime or service disruptions and enhances the overall stability and reliability of the software product. In addition to its technical benefits, CI also has significant cultural and organizational implications for software development teams. By promoting a culture of continuous integration and collaboration, CI encourages teams to work together towards a common goal of delivering high-quality software efficiently and reliably. This collaborative approach fosters trust, accountability, and transparency among team members, leading to improved communication and teamwork. Furthermore, CI encourages teams to embrace agile principles such as iterative development, frequent feedback, and continuous improvement, enabling them to adapt quickly to changing requirements and market conditions. Ultimately, CI empowers teams to deliver value to customers more effectively by reducing lead times, improving code quality, and increasing the frequency of software releases. To implement CI effectively, teams need to establish a robust CI pipeline that automates the build, test, and deployment process for their software projects. A CI pipeline typically consists of several stages, including source code management, build, test, and deployment, each of which is executed sequentially when a code change is committed to the repository. CI pipelines can be configured and managed using a variety of tools and platforms, such as Jenkins, Travis CI, CircleCI, or Azure Pipelines. These tools provide features and capabilities for defining CI pipelines, configuring build and test jobs, and integrating with version control systems and other development tools. For example, in Azure Pipelines, teams can define CI pipelines using YAML or visual designer, specifying the tasks and steps to be executed at each stage of the pipeline. Teams can also leverage built-in features such as triggers, variables, and agent pools to customize and optimize their CI pipelines according to their specific requirements. Once a CI pipeline is set up, developers can commit code changes to the repository with confidence, knowing that their changes will be automatically validated and integrated into the codebase. As code changes progress through the CI pipeline, developers receive feedback about the status of their builds and tests in real-time, enabling them to identify and address issues quickly. Additionally, CI pipelines can be configured to trigger notifications or alerts when builds fail or encounter errors, ensuring that issues are addressed promptly and preventing them from blocking progress. By implementing CI pipelines, teams can streamline their development process, increase productivity, and deliver high-quality software more efficiently. In summary, Continuous Integration (CI) plays a crucial role in modern software development, enabling teams to collaborate effectively, improve code quality, and accelerate the delivery of software products. By automating the build and test process, CI helps teams detect and address integration errors early, reducing the risk of defects and ensuring that software remains in a releasable state at all times. Furthermore, CI serves as the foundation for Continuous Delivery and Continuous Deployment practices, enabling teams to release software updates quickly and reliably. With the right tools, processes, and mindset, teams can harness the power of CI to deliver value to customers more effectively and drive innovation in software development.

A Continuous Integration (CI) workflow is a fundamental aspect of modern software development, providing a structured process for integrating code changes, testing applications, and ensuring the stability and quality of software products. At its core, a CI workflow automates the build, test, and deployment process, enabling teams to deliver software updates quickly and reliably. The CI workflow begins when a developer commits code changes to a shared version control repository, such as Git or SVN, using version control commands such as git add, git commit, and git push. These changes may include bug fixes, new features, or improvements to existing functionality, and are typically committed to a feature branch or development branch to isolate them from the main codebase. Once the code changes are committed, a CI server, such as Jenkins, Travis CI, or Azure Pipelines, automatically detects the changes and triggers a series of build and test jobs to validate the code. The first step in the CI workflow is the build phase, where the CI server retrieves the latest code from the repository and compiles it into executable artifacts, such as binaries, libraries, or container images. This process ensures that the code can be built successfully and that there are no compilation errors or dependencies missing. For example, in a Java project, the CI server may use Maven or Gradle to compile the code and generate a JAR file, while in a Node.js project, it may use npm or Yarn to install dependencies and build the application. Once the code is successfully built, the CI server proceeds to the test phase, where it runs a series of automated tests to verify the correctness and quality of the code. These tests may include unit tests, integration tests, functional tests, or performance tests, depending on the nature of the application and the requirements of the project. For example, in a web application, the CI server may use tools such as Selenium or Cypress to automate browser-based tests, while in a REST API, it may use tools such as Postman or RestAssured to perform API testing. As the tests are executed, the CI server collects and aggregates test results, providing feedback to developers about the success or failure of each test case. If any tests fail, the CI server notifies the development team immediately, allowing them to investigate and address the issues promptly. Once all tests have passed successfully, the CI server proceeds to the deployment phase, where it deploys the built artifacts to a test environment for further validation. This environment may be a staging server, a testing server, or a containerized environment such as Docker or Kubernetes, depending on the requirements of the project. The deployment process may involve copying files to a remote server, provisioning virtual machines or containers, or updating cloud resources such as Azure App Service or AWS Elastic Beanstalk. For example, in a web application, the CI server may use

SSH or SCP commands to transfer files to a remote server, while in a containerized application, it may use Docker commands to build and push container images to a container registry. Once the deployment is complete, the CI server triggers additional tests in the test environment to verify that the application behaves as expected in a production-like environment. These tests may include smoke tests, regression tests, or user acceptance tests, and help ensure that the application is ready for release to production. If any issues are identified during testing, the CI server notifies the development team immediately, allowing them to address the issues before proceeding further. Finally, once all tests have passed successfully in the test environment, the CI server may trigger additional steps such as creating a release package, tagging the code repository with a release version, or notifying stakeholders about the availability of the new release. This marks the end of the CI workflow, and the code changes are now ready to be deployed to production environments. Overall, a CI workflow provides a structured and automated process for integrating code changes, testing applications, and ensuring the quality and stability of software products. By automating repetitive tasks and providing immediate feedback to developers, CI workflows enable teams to deliver software updates quickly and reliably, while maintaining a high level *of quality and reliability. Whether using Jenkins, Travis CI, Azure Pipelines, or another CI server, teams can leverage CI workflows to streamline their development process, improve collaboration, and deliver value to customers more effectively.*

Chapter 2: Configuring CI Pipelines in Azure DevOps

Setting up Continuous Integration (CI) pipelines is a critical step in modern software development, enabling teams to automate the build, test, and deployment process for their applications. The process begins with selecting a CI/CD platform or tool that meets the requirements of the project, such as Jenkins, Travis CI, CircleCI, or Azure Pipelines. Once a CI/CD platform is chosen, the next step is to configure a CI pipeline to automate the tasks involved in building, testing, and deploying the application. This typically involves defining a series of stages or steps that will be executed sequentially when code changes are committed to the repository. For example, in Jenkins, CI pipelines are defined using Jenkinsfiles, which are written in Groovy and stored alongside the codebase in the repository. To create a Jenkinsfile, developers can use a text editor to define the stages, steps, and configuration options for the CI pipeline. Alternatively, Jenkins provides a visual pipeline editor that allows developers to create and edit pipelines using a graphical interface. Once the Jenkinsfile is defined, it is committed to the repository, where it will be detected and executed automatically by the Jenkins server whenever code changes are pushed. In Azure Pipelines, CI pipelines are defined using YAML files, which are stored in the repository alongside the codebase. To create a CI pipeline in Azure Pipelines, developers can define a YAML file with the necessary stages, jobs, and tasks for building, testing, and deploying the application. YAML files provide a simple and flexible syntax for defining CI pipelines, allowing developers to specify parameters, variables, and conditions for each stage of the pipeline. Once the YAML file is defined, it is committed to the repository, where it will be detected and executed automatically by the Azure Pipelines service whenever code changes are pushed. Regardless of the CI/CD platform or tool used, there are several common components and best practices to consider when setting up CI pipelines. One key component is source code management, which involves connecting the CI pipeline to the version control repository where the codebase is stored. This allows the CI pipeline to detect changes to the codebase and trigger automated builds and tests accordingly. Most CI/CD platforms support integration with popular version control systems such as Git, GitHub, Bitbucket, and Azure Repos, allowing developers to choose the repository that best fits their workflow. Another important component of CI pipelines is build automation, which involves compiling the codebase into executable artifacts, such as binaries, libraries, or container images. This process ensures that the code can be built successfully and that there are no compilation errors or dependencies missing. Build automation may involve running build scripts, compiling source code, resolving dependencies, and packaging the application for deployment. In addition to build automation, CI pipelines typically include automated testing to verify the correctness and quality of the code. This may include running unit tests, integration tests, functional tests, or performance tests, depending on the nature of the application and the requirements of the project. Automated testing helps identify bugs, regressions, and other issues early in the development process, reducing the risk of defects and ensuring that the application meets the desired quality standards. Once the code has been built and tested successfully, the next step in the CI pipeline is typically deployment automation, which involves deploying the built artifacts to a test environment for further validation. This may include provisioning infrastructure, configuring services, and deploying applications to cloud platforms such as AWS, Azure, Google Cloud, or on-premises servers. Deployment automation ensures that the application can be deployed consistently and reliably, reducing the likelihood of errors and simplifying the release process. In addition to automating the deployment process, CI pipelines often include post-deployment tasks such as smoke testing, regression testing, and user acceptance testing to verify that the application behaves as expected in a production-like environment. These tests help ensure that the application is ready for release to production and that any issues or regressions are identified and addressed promptly. Finally, CI pipelines typically include notifications and reporting to provide feedback to developers and stakeholders about the status of the pipeline and the quality of the code. This may include sending email notifications, posting messages to collaboration tools such as Slack or Microsoft Teams, or generating reports and dashboards with metrics and insights about the CI pipeline. Notifications and reporting help keep stakeholders informed about the progress of the project and enable teams to identify areas for improvement and optimization in the CI pipeline. Overall, setting up CI pipelines is a critical step in modern software development, enabling teams to automate the build, test, and deployment process for their applications. By defining CI pipelines that integrate seamlessly with the version control repository, automate the build, test, and deployment process, and provide feedback and visibility to developers and stakeholders, teams can accelerate the delivery of software updates, improve code quality, and enhance the overall efficiency and *reliability of the development process. Whether using Jenkins, Azure Pipelines, or another CI/CD platform, teams can leverage CI pipelines to streamline their development workflow, reduce manual effort, and deliver value to customers more quickly and consistently.*

Configuring build agents and environments is a crucial aspect of setting up a Continuous Integration (CI) pipeline, ensuring that code changes are built, tested, and deployed consistently and reliably across different platforms and environments. A build agent, also known as a build server or build agent, is a dedicated machine or virtual machine that executes the tasks defined in the CI pipeline, such as compiling code, running tests, and packaging applications. Build agents play a critical role in the CI process, providing the computing resources and environment needed to execute build and test jobs efficiently. One common approach to configuring build agents is to use a self-hosted agent model, where teams provision and manage their own build agents on-premises or in the cloud. This gives teams greater control and flexibility over the build environment, allowing them to customize the agent configuration to meet their specific requirements. To configure a self-hosted build agent, teams typically install and configure the necessary software and dependencies on a dedicated machine or virtual machine. For example, in a .NET project, teams may install the .NET SDK, Visual Studio, and other development tools on the build agent, while in a Node.js project, they may install Node.js, npm, and other JavaScript libraries and frameworks. Once the build agent is set up, teams can register it with their CI/CD platform or tool, such as Jenkins, Azure Pipelines, or Travis CI, to make it available for executing build and test jobs. This involves configuring authentication credentials, specifying agent capabilities, and defining any additional settings or preferences for the agent. Once registered, the build agent will appear as an available option in the CI/CD platform, allowing teams to select it when configuring their CI pipelines. Another approach to configuring build agents is to use a cloud-based agent model, where teams leverage managed build agents provided by the CI/CD platform or cloud provider. This eliminates the need for teams to provision and manage their own build agents, reducing overhead and simplifying maintenance. To configure a cloud-based build agent, teams typically select the desired agent image or template provided by the CI/CD platform or cloud provider. For example, in Azure Pipelines, teams can choose from a variety of pre-configured agent images for different operating systems and environments, such as Windows, Linux, or macOS. Once selected, the agent image is automatically provisioned and configured by the CI/CD platform, and the build agent is ready to execute build and test jobs. Cloud-based build agents offer several advantages, including scalability, reliability, and consistency. Since the agents are managed by the CI/CD platform or cloud provider, teams can easily scale up or down to meet demand, ensuring that builds and tests are executed quickly and efficiently. Additionally, cloud-based build agents are typically provisioned from clean, isolated environments, reducing the risk of conflicts or inconsistencies between builds. This ensures that builds are executed in a consistent and reproducible manner, regardless of the underlying infrastructure. In addition to configuring build agents, teams must also configure environments for testing and deployment, ensuring that applications are tested and deployed in environments that closely resemble production. This may involve setting up testing environments, staging environments, and production environments, each with its own configuration, data, and dependencies. For example, in a web application project, teams may set up a testing environment with a mock database and sample data for running automated tests, a staging environment with a copy of the production database and configuration for user acceptance testing, and a production environment for deploying the application to end-users. To configure environments, teams typically use infrastructure as code (IaC) tools such as Terraform, Ansible, or ARM templates, which allow them to define and manage infrastructure configuration in a declarative and repeatable manner. Using IaC, teams can define the desired state of the infrastructure, including virtual machines, networks, storage, and other resources, and then use automation to provision and configure the environment automatically. For example, teams can define a Terraform configuration file that specifies the desired resources and settings for a testing environment, such as virtual machines, network security groups, and storage accounts. They can then use the Terraform CLI to apply the configuration, which will create and configure the environment according to the specifications in the file. Once the environment is provisioned, teams can deploy their applications to the environment using deployment automation tools such as Octopus Deploy, Azure DevOps, or AWS CodeDeploy. These tools provide features and capabilities for deploying applications to different environments, managing deployment targets, and executing deployment tasks. For example, in Azure DevOps, teams can define deployment pipelines that specify the steps and actions required to deploy an application to a target environment, such as deploying code changes, running database migrations, and updating configuration settings. Once the *deployment pipeline is defined, teams can trigger it manually or automatically as part of the CI/CD process, ensuring that applications are deployed consistently and reliably across different environments. Overall, configuring build agents and environments is a critical aspect of setting up a CI pipeline, ensuring that code changes are built, tested, and deployed consistently and reliably across different platforms and environments. Whether using self-hosted build agents or cloud-based build agents, teams can leverage automation and infrastructure as code to provision and configure build agents and environments quickly and efficiently. By following best practices and leveraging the right tools and technologies, teams can streamline their CI/CD process, improve collaboration, and deliver value to customers more effectively.*

Chapter 3: Leveraging Automated Testing in CI Pipelines

Automated testing plays a crucial role in Continuous Integration (CI), enabling teams to validate code changes quickly and reliably as part of the CI pipeline. There are various types of automated tests that can be incorporated into the CI process to ensure the quality and stability of software products. One of the most common types of automated tests is unit testing, which involves testing individual units or components of the codebase in isolation. Unit tests are typically written by developers and focus on verifying the behavior of specific functions, methods, or classes. They help ensure that each unit of code behaves as expected and performs its intended functionality correctly. To run unit tests as part of the CI process, teams can use testing frameworks and libraries such as JUnit, NUnit, pytest, or Jasmine, depending on the programming language and technology stack used in the project. For example, in a Java project, developers can use JUnit to write and execute unit tests for their code, while in a Python project, they can use pytest. To execute unit tests in the CI pipeline, teams can use build automation tools such as Maven, Gradle, or npm to run test scripts and generate test reports. For example, in a Maven project, developers can use the mvn test command to execute unit tests and generate test reports in XML format, which can then be parsed and displayed in the CI pipeline. Another type of automated test commonly used in CI is integration testing, which involves testing the interactions and integration between different components or modules of the application. Integration tests focus on verifying that individual units of code work together correctly and communicate with each other as expected. They help identify issues such as interface mismatches, data format inconsistencies, and communication errors between components. To run integration tests as part of the CI process, teams can use testing frameworks and libraries such as TestNG, Mockito, Selenium, or Postman, depending on the nature of the tests and the technology stack used in the project. For example, in a Java project, developers can use TestNG and Mockito to write and execute integration tests for their code, while in a web application project, they can use Selenium and Postman to automate browser-based and API tests. To execute integration tests in the CI pipeline, teams can use build automation tools such as Maven, Gradle, or npm to run test scripts and generate test reports, similar to how unit tests are executed. For example, in a Maven project, developers can use the mvn verify command to execute integration tests and generate test reports in XML format, which can then be parsed and displayed in the CI pipeline. In addition to unit testing and integration testing, another type of automated test commonly used in CI is functional testing, which involves testing the application as a whole to verify its functionality and behavior from an end-user perspective. Functional tests focus on testing the application's user interface, user interactions, and business logic to ensure that it meets the requirements and specifications defined for it. To run functional tests as part of the CI process, teams can use testing frameworks and tools such as Selenium WebDriver, Cypress, or Cucumber, depending on the nature of the tests and the technology stack used in the project. For example, in a web application project, developers can use Selenium WebDriver to automate browser-based tests that simulate user interactions and verify the functionality of the application's user interface. To execute functional tests in the CI pipeline, teams can use build automation tools such as Maven, Gradle, or npm to run test scripts and generate test reports, similar to how unit tests and integration tests are executed. For example, in a Maven project, developers can use the mvn verify command to execute functional tests and generate test reports in XML format, which can then be parsed and displayed in the CI pipeline. In addition to unit testing, integration testing, and functional testing, teams may also incorporate other types of automated tests into the CI process, such as performance testing, security testing, and accessibility testing, depending on the requirements and constraints of the project. Performance testing involves testing the performance and scalability of the application under various load conditions to ensure that it can handle the expected volume of traffic and users. Security testing involves testing the application for vulnerabilities and weaknesses that could be exploited by attackers to compromise its integrity, confidentiality, or availability. Accessibility testing involves testing the application for compliance with accessibility standards and guidelines, ensuring that it is usable and accessible to users with disabilities. To run these types of automated tests as part of the CI process, teams can use specialized testing tools and frameworks such as JMeter, OWASP ZAP, or Axe, depending on the nature of the tests and the technology stack used in the project. For example, in a web application project, developers can use JMeter to automate performance tests that simulate user interactions and measure the application's response time and throughput under various load conditions. To execute these types of tests in the CI pipeline, teams can use build automation tools such as Maven, Gradle, or npm to run test scripts and generate test *reports, similar to how other types of automated tests are executed. For example, in a Maven project, developers can use the mvn verify command to execute performance tests and generate test reports in XML format, which can then be parsed and displayed in the CI pipeline. In summary, there are various types of automated tests that can be incorporated into the CI process to ensure the quality and stability of software products. By running unit tests, integration tests, functional tests, and other types of automated tests as part of the CI pipeline, teams can detect and address issues early in the development process, reduce the risk of defects, and deliver high-quality software products more efficiently and reliably. Whether using testing frameworks and libraries such as JUnit, TestNG, Selenium, or specialized testing tools and frameworks for performance testing, security testing, and accessibility testing, teams can leverage automated testing to validate code changes quickly and reliably as part of the CI process. By following best practices and incorporating automated tests into their CI pipelines, teams can accelerate the delivery of software updates, improve code quality, and enhance the overall efficiency and reliability of the development process. Integrating testing frameworks into Continuous Integration (CI) pipelines is essential for ensuring the quality and reliability of software products* throughout the development process. Testing frameworks provide developers with tools and libraries for writing and executing automated tests, enabling them to validate code changes quickly and consistently. One of the most widely used testing frameworks is JUnit, a unit testing framework for Java applications that allows developers to write and execute unit tests for their code. To integrate JUnit into a CI pipeline, developers typically include the JUnit library as a dependency in their project's build configuration file, such as a Maven pom.xml file or a Gradle build.gradle file. For example, in a Maven project, developers can add the JUnit dependency to the <dependencies> section of the pom.xml file:

xmlCopy code

<dependency>   <groupId>junit</groupId> <artifactId>junit</artifactId>

<version>4.12</version>   <scope>test</scope> </dependency>

Once the JUnit dependency is added, developers can write unit tests using the JUnit framework and execute them as part of the Maven build process. For example, developers can use the mvn test command to execute JUnit tests and generate test reports in XML format, which can then be parsed and displayed in the CI pipeline. In addition to JUnit, there are many other testing frameworks available for different programming languages and technology stacks, such as NUnit for .NET applications, pytest for Python applications, and Jasmine for JavaScript applications. To integrate these testing frameworks into CI pipelines, developers follow a similar process of including the framework's library or package as a dependency in their project's build configuration file and executing tests using the appropriate commands or scripts. For example, in a .NET project using NUnit, developers can include the NUnit framework as a NuGet package and use the dotnet test command to execute NUnit tests. Similarly, in a Python project using pytest, developers can include the pytest framework as a dependency in their requirements.txt file and use the pytest command to execute pytest tests. By integrating testing frameworks into CI pipelines, developers can automate the process of running tests and generating test reports, enabling them to identify and address issues quickly and efficiently. In addition to unit testing frameworks, CI pipelines often include integration testing frameworks for testing the interactions and integration between different components or modules of the application. One popular integration testing framework is TestNG, a testing framework for Java applications that allows developers to write and execute integration tests for their code. To integrate TestNG into a CI pipeline, developers follow a similar process to that of integrating JUnit, by including the TestNG library as a dependency in their project's build configuration file and executing tests using the appropriate commands or scripts. For example, in a Maven project, developers can add the TestNG dependency to the pom.xml file and use the mvn test command to execute TestNG tests. In addition to unit and integration testing frameworks, CI pipelines may also include functional testing frameworks for testing the application as a whole to verify its functionality and behavior from an end-user perspective. One popular functional testing framework is Selenium WebDriver, a web browser automation tool that allows developers to automate browser-based tests for their web applications. To integrate Selenium WebDriver into a CI pipeline, developers typically include the Selenium WebDriver library as a dependency in their project's build configuration file and use the appropriate WebDriver drivers for the browsers they want to test. For example, in a Maven project, developers can add the Selenium WebDriver dependency to the pom.xml file and include the appropriate WebDriver drivers for Chrome, Firefox, or other browsers. They can then write Selenium WebDriver tests using the appropriate programming language bindings (e.g., Java, Python) and execute them as part of the Maven build process. By integrating testing frameworks into CI pipelines, developers can *automate the process of running tests and generating test reports, enabling them to identify and address issues quickly and efficiently. This helps ensure the quality and reliability of software products throughout the development process, leading to faster delivery times, fewer defects, and improved customer satisfaction. Overall, integrating testing frameworks into CI pipelines is a critical aspect of modern software development, enabling teams to automate testing processes, improve code quality, and deliver high-quality software products more efficiently and reliably. Whether using JUnit, TestNG, Selenium WebDriver, or other testing frameworks, teams can leverage automated testing to validate code changes quickly and consistently as part of their CI pipelines. By following best practices and integrating testing frameworks into their CI pipelines, teams can accelerate the delivery of software updates, reduce manual effort, and deliver value to customers more effectively.*

Chapter 4: Advanced CI Techniques: Branch Policies and Triggers

Branching strategies play a crucial role in the success of Continuous Integration (CI) pipelines, as they determine how code changes are managed and integrated into the main codebase. One commonly used branching strategy is the feature branch model, where each feature or task is developed in its own branch before being merged into the main codebase. To implement the feature branch model, developers create a new branch for each feature or task they are working on, typically naming the branch according to the feature or task it represents. For example, a developer working on a new login feature might create a branch named "feature/login" to develop and test the changes related to that feature. Once the changes are complete and tested, the developer merges the feature branch into the main codebase, typically using a pull request or merge request mechanism provided by the version control system. This allows other team members to review the changes and provide feedback before they are merged into the main codebase. Another branching strategy commonly used in CI pipelines is the Gitflow model, which defines a strict branching model with separate branches for features, releases, and hotfixes. In the Gitflow model, development work is typically done in feature branches, which are branched off from the "develop" branch and merged back into it once the feature is complete. Once the development work is complete and tested, a release branch is created from the "develop" branch, which is used to prepare the code for deployment to production. Once the release branch is tested and ready, it is merged into the "master" branch, which represents the main codebase and is deployed to production. In addition to feature branches and release branches, the Gitflow model also includes branches for hotfixes, which are used to address critical issues or bugs in production code. To implement the Gitflow model, developers follow a set of branching conventions and guidelines, such as naming conventions for branches and rules for merging and deploying code changes. For example, developers might use the git-flow CLI tool to initialize and manage the Gitflow branching model in their repository, using commands such as git flow feature start to create a new feature branch and git flow feature finish to merge it back into the "develop" branch. While the feature branch model and Gitflow model are two common branching strategies used in CI pipelines, there are many other variations and hybrid models that teams can use depending on their specific requirements and workflows. For example, some teams may use a trunk-based development model, where all development work is done directly on the main branch (e.g., "master" or "main"), with feature flags or toggles used to isolate and control the release of new features. Other teams may use a release branch model, where each release is developed and tested in its own branch before being merged into the main codebase. Regardless of the branching strategy used, the key principles of CI - such as frequent integration, automated testing, and continuous feedback - remain the same, enabling teams to deliver high-quality software products more efficiently and reliably. By choosing the right branching strategy and following best practices for CI, teams can streamline their development process, reduce conflicts and integration issues, and deliver value to customers more effectively. Overall, branching strategies are an integral part of CI pipelines, providing a framework for managing code changes and ensuring that development work is integrated and tested smoothly. Whether using the feature branch model, Gitflow model, or another branching strategy, teams can leverage branching conventions and tools to streamline their development workflow and deliver high-quality software products more efficiently and reliably.

Configuring trigger rules for Continuous Integration (CI) pipelines is essential for automating the process of building, testing, and deploying code changes in response to specific events or conditions. Trigger rules define when a CI pipeline should be executed based on changes to the codebase, such as commits to version control repositories, pull requests, or scheduled intervals. One common trigger rule used in CI pipelines is the "on push" trigger, which initiates the pipeline whenever new code changes are pushed to the version control repository. To configure an "on push" trigger rule in CI pipelines, developers typically specify the branches or tags that should trigger the pipeline execution, along with any additional conditions or filters, such as branch name patterns or file paths. For example, in Azure Pipelines, developers can define a trigger section in their pipeline configuration file (e.g., azure-pipelines.yml) and specify the branches that should trigger the pipeline:

yamlCopy code

trigger: branches: include: - main - feature/*

This configuration will trigger the pipeline whenever code changes are pushed to the "main" branch or any branch starting with "feature/". Another common trigger rule used in CI pipelines is the "on pull request" trigger, which initiates the pipeline whenever a new pull request is opened or updated in the version control repository. To configure an "on pull request" trigger rule, developers typically specify the branches that should trigger the pipeline execution, along with any additional conditions or filters, such as branch name patterns or file paths. For example, in GitHub Actions, developers can define a workflow file (e.g., .github/workflows/main.yml) and specify the pull_request event in the on section:

yamlCopy code

on: pull_request: branches: - main

This configuration will trigger the workflow whenever a new pull request is opened or updated for the "main" branch. In addition to "on push" and "on pull request" triggers, CI pipelines may also include other trigger rules based on specific events or conditions, such as scheduled triggers, manual triggers, or triggers based on external events. Scheduled triggers initiate the pipeline execution at specified intervals, such as daily or weekly, to perform tasks such as automated backups, cleanup jobs, or periodic checks. To configure a scheduled trigger rule, developers typically specify the schedule or cron expression in the trigger section of the pipeline configuration file. For example, in GitLab CI/CD, developers can define a schedule section in their pipeline configuration file (e.g., .gitlab-ci.yml) and specify the cron expression for the desired schedule:

yamlCopy code

schedule: cron: "0 0 * * *"

This configuration will trigger the pipeline every day at midnight. Manual triggers initiate the pipeline execution manually by users or automated systems, allowing developers to control when and how the pipeline is executed. To configure a manual trigger rule, developers typically specify a manual keyword in the trigger section of the pipeline configuration file. For example, in Jenkins Pipeline, developers can define an input step in their pipeline script to prompt users for manual approval before proceeding with the pipeline execution:

```groovy
groovyCopy code
pipeline { agent any stages { stage('Build') { steps {
echo 'Building...' } } } post { always { input "Deploy to
production?" } } }
```

This configuration will pause the pipeline execution and prompt users to confirm whether they want to deploy to production before proceeding. Triggers based on external events initiate the pipeline execution in response to events from external systems or services, such as webhooks, API calls, or third-party integrations. To configure a trigger rule based on an external event, developers typically specify the event type and any required parameters or conditions in the trigger section of the pipeline configuration file. For example, in Azure Pipelines, developers can define a trigger section in their pipeline configuration file (e.g., azure-pipelines.yml) *and specify the event type and endpoint URL for the external event:*

yamlCopy code

trigger: batch: true branches: include: - '' paths: exclude: - README.md*

This configuration will trigger the pipeline whenever a webhook event is received from the specified endpoint URL. Overall, configuring trigger rules for CI pipelines is a critical aspect of automating the software development process, enabling teams to build, test, and deploy code changes quickly and reliably in response to specific events or conditions. By defining trigger rules based on "on push" events, "on pull request" events, scheduled intervals, manual actions, or external events, teams can streamline their development workflow, improve collaboration, and deliver value to customers more effectively. Whether using GitLab CI/CD, GitHub Actions, Jenkins Pipeline, or Azure Pipelines, teams can leverage trigger rules to automate the execution of CI pipelines and ensure that code changes are integrated and tested consistently and reliably. By following best practices and incorporating trigger rules into their CI pipelines, teams can accelerate the delivery of software updates, reduce manual effort, and deliver high-quality software products more efficiently and reliably.

Chapter 5: Introduction to Continuous Deployment (CD) Concepts

Continuous Deployment (CD) pipelines are an integral part of modern software development practices, enabling teams to automate the process of deploying code changes to production environments quickly and reliably. The primary goal of a CD pipeline is to streamline the deployment process, reducing manual effort and minimizing the risk of errors or downtime. CD pipelines are typically composed of a series of stages or steps that automate the process of building, testing, and deploying code changes to production environments. One of the key principles of CD pipelines is to ensure that code changes are deployed to production environments as soon as they pass automated tests and meet predefined quality criteria. To achieve this, CD pipelines often include automated testing processes, such as unit tests, integration tests, and end-to-end tests, to verify the functionality and stability of code changes before they are deployed to production. By automating the testing process, CD pipelines can identify and address issues early in the development cycle, reducing the risk of defects and ensuring that only high-quality code changes are deployed to production environments. In addition to automated testing processes, CD pipelines may also include other stages or steps to automate tasks such as code compilation, dependency management, database migrations, and environment provisioning. These stages help streamline the deployment process and ensure that code changes are deployed consistently and reliably across different environments. One common practice in CD pipelines is to use version control systems to manage code changes and trigger pipeline executions automatically whenever new code changes are pushed to the repository. This allows teams to integrate code changes into the deployment process seamlessly and ensures that changes are deployed to production environments quickly and efficiently. To set up a CD pipeline, teams typically use CI/CD tools and platforms such as Jenkins, GitLab CI/CD, CircleCI, or Azure DevOps, which provide features and functionalities for automating the deployment process. These tools allow teams to define pipeline configurations using YAML or DSL (Domain-Specific Language) files, specifying the stages, steps, and conditions for deploying code changes to production environments. For example, in Jenkins, teams can create a Jenkinsfile to define the stages and steps of the CD pipeline, specifying the build, test, and deploy stages using declarative or scripted syntax. Similarly, in GitLab CI/CD, teams can define a

.gitlab-ci.yml file to configure the pipeline stages and steps, specifying the jobs, dependencies, and triggers for deploying code changes to production environments. Once the CD pipeline is defined, teams can trigger pipeline executions manually or automatically whenever new code changes are pushed to the repository. By automating the deployment process, CD pipelines help teams reduce the time and effort required to deploy code changes to production environments, enabling them to deliver value to customers more quickly and reliably. In addition to automating the deployment process, CD pipelines also help teams improve the overall quality and reliability of their software products by ensuring that code changes are thoroughly tested before they are deployed to production environments. This helps reduce the risk of defects and downtime, improving the user experience and increasing customer satisfaction. Overall, CD pipelines are an essential tool for modern software development teams, enabling them to automate the deployment process, improve code quality, and deliver value to customers more efficiently and reliably. By adopting CD pipelines as part of their development process, teams can streamline the deployment process, reduce manual effort, and accelerate the delivery of software updates to production environments.
Continuous Integration (CI) and Continuous

Deployment (CD) are two essential practices in modern software development, but they serve distinct purposes within the development lifecycle. CI focuses on integrating code changes into a shared repository frequently, allowing developers to detect and fix integration errors early in the development process. CD, on the other hand, extends CI by automating the process of deploying code changes to production environments. While both CI and CD aim to improve the development process and deliver high-quality software products, they differ in their scope and objectives. CI pipelines typically include stages for code compilation, unit testing, and static code analysis, among other tasks. These pipelines are triggered automatically whenever new code changes are pushed to the version control repository, ensuring that changes are integrated and tested continuously. To set up a CI pipeline, teams use CI/CD tools such as Jenkins, GitLab CI/CD, or Azure DevOps, which allow them to define pipeline configurations using YAML or DSL files. These configurations specify the stages, steps, and conditions for building, testing, and validating code changes as part of the CI process. Once a CI pipeline is defined, it automatically triggers pipeline executions whenever new code changes are pushed to the repository, providing feedback to developers quickly and enabling them to identify and address issues early in the development cycle. By automating the integration and testing process, CI pipelines help teams reduce the risk of integration errors, improve code quality, and accelerate the delivery of software updates. CD, on the other hand, focuses on automating the process of deploying code changes to production environments, enabling teams to release new features and updates to customers quickly and reliably. While CI pipelines ensure that code changes are integrated and tested frequently, CD pipelines extend this process by automating the deployment process and delivering code changes to production environments seamlessly. CD pipelines typically include stages for building artifacts, running automated tests, deploying changes to staging environments, and promoting changes to production environments, among other tasks. These pipelines are triggered automatically whenever new code changes are integrated and tested successfully as part of the CI process. To set up a CD pipeline, teams use CI/CD tools such as Jenkins, GitLab CI/CD, or Azure DevOps, which provide features and functionalities for automating the deployment process. These tools allow teams to define pipeline configurations using YAML or DSL files, specifying the stages, steps, and conditions for deploying code changes to production environments. Once a CD pipeline is defined, it automatically triggers pipeline executions whenever new code changes are integrated and tested successfully, ensuring that changes are deployed to production environments quickly and reliably. By automating the deployment process, CD pipelines help teams reduce the time and effort required to release new features and updates to customers, enabling them to deliver value more efficiently and reliably. While CI and CD are distinct practices, they are often used together as part of a unified CI/CD pipeline, which combines the benefits of both practices to streamline the development and deployment process. In a CI/CD pipeline, code changes are integrated, tested, and deployed automatically, providing teams with continuous feedback and enabling them to deliver high-quality software products quickly and reliably. By adopting CI/CD pipelines as part of their development process, teams can accelerate the delivery of software updates, reduce manual effort, and improve the overall quality and reliability of their software products.

Chapter 6: Implementing CD Pipelines in Azure DevOps

Creating Continuous Deployment (CD) pipelines is a crucial step in modern software development, enabling teams to automate the process of deploying code changes to production environments quickly and reliably. CD pipelines are an extension of Continuous Integration (CI) pipelines, adding stages and steps to automate the deployment process after code changes have been integrated and tested successfully. To create CD pipelines, teams typically use CI/CD tools and platforms such as Jenkins, GitLab CI/CD, CircleCI, or Azure DevOps, which provide features and functionalities for defining, configuring, and executing CD pipelines. These tools allow teams to define pipeline configurations using YAML or DSL files, specifying the stages, steps, and conditions for deploying code changes to production environments. For example, in Jenkins, teams can create a Jenkinsfile to define the stages and steps of the CD pipeline, specifying the deployment tasks and conditions using declarative or scripted syntax. Similarly, in GitLab CI/CD, teams can define a .gitlab-ci.yml file to configure the pipeline stages and steps, specifying the jobs, dependencies, and triggers for deploying code changes to production environments. Once the CD pipeline is defined, teams can trigger pipeline executions manually or automatically whenever new code changes are pushed to the version control repository. By automating the deployment process, CD pipelines help teams reduce the time and effort required to release new features and updates to customers, enabling them to deliver value more efficiently and reliably. In addition to automating the deployment process, CD pipelines also help teams improve the overall quality and reliability of their software products by ensuring that code changes are thoroughly tested before they are deployed to production environments. This helps reduce the risk of defects and downtime, improving the user experience and increasing customer satisfaction. CD pipelines typically include stages for building artifacts, running automated tests, deploying changes to staging environments, and promoting changes to production environments, among other tasks. These stages help streamline the deployment process and ensure that code changes are deployed consistently and reliably across different environments. One common practice in CD pipelines is to use version control systems to manage code changes and trigger pipeline executions automatically whenever new code changes are pushed to the repository. This allows teams to integrate code changes into the deployment process *seamlessly and ensures that changes are deployed to production environments quickly and efficiently. To set up a CD pipeline, teams typically follow a set of best practices and guidelines for defining, configuring, and executing CD pipelines. These practices include modularizing pipelines into reusable components, using infrastructure as code (IaC) to define and provision deployment environments, implementing automated testing processes to validate code changes before they are deployed, and implementing rollback mechanisms to revert changes in case of deployment failures. By following these best practices, teams can streamline the deployment process, reduce manual effort, and deliver high-quality software products more efficiently and reliably. Overall, creating CD pipelines is an essential aspect of modern software development, enabling teams to automate the deployment process and deliver value to customers more quickly and reliably. By adopting CD pipelines as part of their development process, teams can accelerate the delivery of software updates, reduce manual effort, and improve the overall quality and reliability of their software products.*

Defining deployment environments is a critical aspect of setting up Continuous Deployment (CD) pipelines, as it provides a structured approach for deploying code changes to different stages of the software development lifecycle. Deployment environments represent the various stages through which code changes progress before reaching production, such as development, testing, staging, and production environments. Each environment serves a specific purpose and is used for different types of testing and validation activities. The development environment is typically the first environment in the deployment pipeline and is used by developers to test their code changes locally before pushing them to the version control repository. To set up a development environment, developers can use local development environments on their machines, such as Docker containers or virtual machines, to replicate the production environment and test their code changes in a controlled environment. Once the code changes are ready for testing, developers push them to the version control repository, triggering the CI/CD pipeline to deploy the changes to the testing environment. The testing environment is used for automated and manual testing of code changes, including unit tests, integration tests, and end-to-end tests. To set up a testing environment, teams typically provision dedicated environments or use cloud-based services such as AWS, Azure, or Google Cloud Platform to create and manage testing environments dynamically. This allows teams to spin up testing environments on-demand, run tests in parallel, and scale resources based on testing requirements. Once the code changes pass all tests in the testing environment, they are promoted to the staging environment for further validation and acceptance testing. The staging environment closely resembles the production environment and is used to validate code changes in a production-like environment before deploying them to production. To set up a staging environment, teams typically replicate the production environment using infrastructure as code (IaC) tools such as Terraform or AWS CloudFormation, ensuring consistency and reproducibility across environments. This allows teams to deploy code changes to the staging environment with confidence, knowing that they will behave similarly to production. Once the code changes are validated in the staging environment, they are promoted to the production environment for final deployment. The production environment is the live environment where the code changes are deployed for end-users to access and use. To set up a production environment, teams provision infrastructure resources such as servers, databases, and networking components in a secure and scalable manner, using best practices and security guidelines. This ensures that the production environment is reliable, performant, and resilient to failures, minimizing downtime and ensuring a positive user experience. Throughout the deployment pipeline, it's essential to maintain consistency and traceability across environments, ensuring that code changes behave predictably as they progress through the pipeline. To achieve this, teams can use version control systems to manage infrastructure configurations and deployment scripts, ensuring that changes are tracked and auditable over time. Additionally, teams can implement automated testing processes and quality gates to validate code changes before promoting them to the next environment, reducing the risk of defects and failures in production. By defining deployment environments and following best practices for infrastructure provisioning and deployment automation, teams can streamline the deployment process, reduce manual effort, and deliver high-quality software products more efficiently and reliably. Overall, defining deployment environments is a crucial step in setting up CD pipelines, enabling teams to deploy code changes to production environments quickly and confidently, while maintaining consistency and reliability across environments.

Chapter 7: Blue-Green Deployments and Deployment Strategies

Blue-green deployment is a deployment strategy used in software development to minimize downtime and reduce the risk associated with deploying new code changes to production environments. The basic concept of blue-green deployment involves running two identical production environments, referred to as blue and green, in parallel. To initiate a blue-green deployment, teams first deploy the new version of the application to the "green" environment, while the existing version of the application continues to run in the "blue" environment. This allows teams to test the new version of the application in isolation without affecting end-users or interrupting service. Once the new version of the application has been deployed to the green environment and tested thoroughly, teams can switch traffic from the blue environment to the green environment, directing users to the new version of the application seamlessly. This switch is typically performed using a load balancer or DNS routing rules, which redirect incoming traffic from the blue environment to the green environment. By directing traffic to the green environment gradually, teams can monitor the performance and stability of the new version of the application in a real-world production environment, ensuring that it meets performance and reliability requirements before fully deploying it to all users. If any issues or defects are identified during the green environment testing phase, teams can easily roll back to the blue environment by reverting the traffic routing rules, restoring the previous version of the application and minimizing the impact on end-users. This ability to roll back quickly and seamlessly is one of the key benefits of blue-green deployment, as it allows teams to mitigate risks and recover from deployment failures or issues rapidly. Another benefit of blue-green deployment is its ability to eliminate downtime during the deployment process, as both the blue and green environments are running simultaneously, allowing users to access the application without interruption. This is particularly important for mission-critical applications and services that require high availability and uptime. By eliminating downtime, teams can deploy code changes to production environments more frequently and confidently, accelerating the delivery of new features and updates to users. Additionally, blue-green deployment enables teams to perform A/B testing and canary releases, allowing them to compare the performance and user experience of different application versions in real-time. This is achieved by directing a portion of the incoming traffic to the green environment while keeping the majority of traffic on the blue environment, allowing teams to gather feedback and data on the new version of the application before fully rolling it out to all users. To implement blue-green deployment, teams can use CI/CD tools and platforms such as Jenkins, GitLab CI/CD, or Azure DevOps, which provide features and functionalities for automating the deployment process and managing traffic routing rules. For example, in Kubernetes, teams can use a service object with a load balancer or ingress controller to manage traffic routing between blue and green environments, specifying the desired traffic distribution and failover behavior. Additionally, teams can use deployment strategies such as rolling updates or canary deployments to control the rate at which traffic is shifted between environments, ensuring a smooth and controlled deployment process. Overall, blue-green deployment offers several benefits for software development teams, including reduced downtime, minimized risk, increased flexibility, and improved user experience. By leveraging blue-green deployment as part of their deployment strategy, teams can deploy code changes to production environments more frequently and reliably, delivering value to users more efficiently and effectively.

Implementing blue-green deployments in Azure

DevOps is a powerful technique for deploying code changes to production environments seamlessly and with minimal downtime. Azure DevOps provides robust features and capabilities to support blue-green deployments, allowing teams to automate the deployment process and ensure a smooth transition between different versions of their applications. One of the key benefits of using Azure DevOps for blue-green deployments is its integration with Azure services, which provide a scalable and reliable platform for hosting applications and managing deployment environments. To implement blue-green deployments in Azure DevOps, teams first need to define their deployment environments, including the blue and green environments, which will run different versions of the application simultaneously. This can be done using Azure Resource Manager (ARM) templates to provision infrastructure resources such as virtual machines, databases, and networking components. Once the deployment environments are defined, teams can create release pipelines in Azure DevOps to automate the deployment process. Release pipelines in Azure DevOps allow teams to define the stages, tasks, and conditions for deploying code changes to different environments, including the blue and green environments. Teams can use the Azure CLI (Command-Line Interface) to deploy resources and configure settings in Azure, such as creating virtual machines, deploying application code, and updating DNS routing rules to direct traffic between blue and green environments. Additionally, teams can use Azure DevOps tasks and extensions to integrate with other Azure services, such as Azure App Service, Azure Kubernetes Service (AKS), and Azure Traffic Manager, to manage deployment resources and automate the deployment process further. One approach to implementing blue-green deployments in Azure DevOps is to use deployment slots in Azure App Service, which allow teams to deploy different versions of their application to separate slots within the same App Service instance. Teams can configure a production slot (blue environment) and a staging slot (green environment) within the same App Service instance and deploy code changes to the staging slot first. Once the code changes have been tested and validated in the staging slot, teams can swap the staging and production slots using Azure CLI commands or Azure DevOps tasks, directing traffic from the blue environment to the green environment seamlessly. This approach allows teams to perform blue-green deployments without provisioning additional infrastructure resources, making it cost-effective and efficient. Another approach to implementing blue-green deployments in Azure DevOps is to use Azure Kubernetes Service (AKS), which provides a scalable and flexible platform for deploying containerized applications.

Teams can create multiple Kubernetes namespaces for different versions of their application, such as blue and green namespaces, and deploy code changes to the green namespace first. Once the code changes have been validated in the green namespace, teams can update the DNS routing rules using Azure Traffic Manager or Azure DNS to direct traffic from the blue namespace to the green namespace gradually. This approach allows teams to leverage the scalability and resilience of Kubernetes while implementing blue-green deployments in a cloud-native environment. Regardless of the approach chosen, it's essential for teams to automate the deployment process as much as possible and perform thorough testing and validation before directing traffic to the new version of the application. Azure DevOps provides robust features and capabilities to support blue-green deployments, allowing teams to deploy code changes to production environments quickly and reliably, while minimizing downtime and risk. By leveraging Azure DevOps for blue-green deployments, teams can accelerate the delivery of new features and updates to users, improve the overall quality and reliability of their applications, and deliver value more efficiently and effectively.

Chapter 8: Monitoring and Rollback Strategies for CD Pipelines

Monitoring Continuous Deployment (CD) pipelines is crucial for ensuring the reliability, performance, and stability of production environments during the deployment process. CD pipelines automate the deployment of code changes to production environments, but monitoring is essential to detect and respond to issues or failures that may occur during the deployment process. Monitoring CD pipelines involves tracking various metrics and indicators, such as deployment success rates, deployment duration, error rates, and resource utilization, to assess the health and performance of the deployment process. Teams can use monitoring tools and platforms such as Azure Monitor, Prometheus, Grafana, or Datadog to collect, visualize, and analyze these metrics in real-time. Azure Monitor is a comprehensive monitoring solution provided by Microsoft Azure, which allows teams to monitor the performance and availability of applications and services deployed on Azure. To monitor CD pipelines using Azure Monitor, teams can configure custom metrics and alerts to track deployment-related metrics such as deployment success rates, deployment duration, and error rates. Teams can use Azure CLI commands to create custom metrics and alerts in Azure Monitor, specifying the thresholds and conditions for triggering alerts based on predefined criteria. For example, teams can create alerts to notify them when the deployment success rate falls below a certain threshold or when the deployment duration exceeds a specified time limit. By monitoring deployment-related metrics and setting up alerts in Azure Monitor, teams can proactively detect and respond to issues or failures in CD pipelines, minimizing downtime and ensuring the reliability of production environments. In addition to tracking deployment-related metrics, teams can also monitor the health and performance of underlying infrastructure resources such as virtual machines, databases, and networking components. Teams can use Azure Monitor to collect telemetry data from these resources, such as CPU utilization, memory usage, disk I/O, and network traffic, and analyze this data to identify performance bottlenecks or resource constraints that may impact the deployment process. By monitoring infrastructure resources in real-time, teams can detect and mitigate issues or failures that may affect the stability and reliability of production environments during the deployment process. Another aspect of monitoring CD pipelines is tracking the progress and status of deployment tasks and stages within the pipeline. Teams can use Azure DevOps to visualize and monitor the progress of deployment pipelines, including the status of individual tasks, the duration of each stage, and the overall progress of the deployment process. Azure DevOps provides built-in dashboards and reports to track deployment pipelines' status, allowing teams to monitor deployment progress in real-time and identify any bottlenecks or issues that may arise during the deployment process. By monitoring deployment pipelines' status and progress, teams can identify and address issues quickly, ensuring that code changes are deployed to production environments efficiently and reliably. Additionally, teams can use logging and tracing to capture detailed information and diagnostics data during the deployment process. Teams can use tools such as Azure Application Insights, Elasticsearch, or Splunk to collect and analyze logs, traces, and events generated by applications and services deployed in production environments. By analyzing logs and traces, teams can gain insights into application performance, identify errors or exceptions, and troubleshoot issues that may occur during the deployment process. By monitoring CD pipelines and production environments effectively, teams can ensure the reliability, performance, and availability of applications and services deployed in production environments. Monitoring CD pipelines allows teams to detect and respond to issues or failures quickly, *minimize downtime, and deliver high-quality software products to end-users efficiently and reliably.*

Rollback strategies and best practices are essential components of any deployment process, ensuring that teams can revert to a stable state in case of deployment failures or issues. One common rollback strategy is to use a blue-green deployment approach, where two identical production environments, known as blue and green, run in parallel. If issues are detected in the green environment after deploying new changes, teams can quickly revert to the blue environment, which contains the previous version of the application. This rollback process involves updating DNS routing rules or load balancer configurations to redirect traffic from the green environment to the blue environment seamlessly. By leveraging blue-green deployment, teams can minimize downtime and ensure a smooth transition between different versions of the application. Another rollback strategy is to use feature toggles or feature flags, which allow teams to enable or disable specific features or changes in real-time without redeploying the application. If issues are detected after deploying new changes, teams can simply disable the problematic feature or toggle, reverting the application to a stable state without rolling back the entire deployment. Feature toggles provide flexibility and granular control over the deployment process, allowing teams to mitigate risks and recover from failures quickly. In addition to using blue-green deployment and feature toggles, teams can also implement automated rollback mechanisms as part of their deployment pipelines. For example, teams can configure CI/CD tools such as Azure DevOps or Jenkins to automatically roll back deployments if predefined conditions or thresholds are met, such as a high error rate or a significant increase in response times. This automated rollback process helps teams respond to deployment failures or issues proactively, minimizing downtime and ensuring the reliability of production environments. To implement automated rollback mechanisms, teams can use scripting or CLI commands to trigger rollback actions, such as reverting code changes, restoring database backups, or rolling back configuration changes. For example, in Azure DevOps, teams can use Azure CLI commands or PowerShell scripts to revert deployments by redeploying a previous version of the application from a release artifact or source control repository. By scripting rollback actions, teams can automate the rollback process and ensure consistency and reliability across deployments. When defining rollback strategies and best practices, it's essential for teams to consider the impact of rollbacks on data consistency, user *experience, and application state. Rollbacks should be performed carefully to avoid data loss or corruption and to minimize disruption to end-users. Teams should also document rollback procedures and communicate them to stakeholders to ensure that everyone is aware of the rollback process and knows how to execute it in case of emergencies. Additionally, teams should conduct regular rollback drills and exercises to test the effectiveness of rollback procedures and validate their ability to recover from failures quickly. By practicing rollback procedures regularly, teams can build confidence in their deployment process and ensure that they are prepared to respond to deployment failures or issues effectively. Overall, rollback strategies and best practices are essential for ensuring the reliability and stability of production environments during the deployment process. By leveraging techniques such as blue-green deployment, feature toggles, and automated rollback mechanisms, teams can minimize downtime, mitigate risks, and deliver high-quality software products to end-users efficiently and reliably.*

Chapter 9: Infrastructure as Code (IaC) and CD in Azure DevOps

Introduction to Infrastructure as Code (IaC) revolutionizes the way infrastructure is managed and provisioned in modern software development. IaC is a practice that enables the provisioning and management of infrastructure resources using code and automation techniques. With IaC, infrastructure components such as virtual machines, networks, storage, and other resources are defined and managed through code files, rather than manually configuring them through a graphical user interface or command-line interface. This approach offers numerous benefits, including repeatability, consistency, and scalability. One of the key advantages of IaC is the ability to treat infrastructure as software, applying software engineering principles such as version control, code review, and testing to infrastructure configurations. By defining infrastructure resources as code, teams can maintain version history, track changes, and collaborate more effectively on infrastructure changes. Additionally, IaC allows teams to automate the provisioning and deployment of infrastructure resources, reducing manual effort and eliminating human error. This automation streamlines the deployment process, accelerates time-to-market, and improves the overall reliability of infrastructure deployments. In traditional infrastructure management approaches, such as manual configuration or script-based provisioning, making changes to infrastructure configurations can be complex and error-prone. With IaC, changes to infrastructure configurations are made through code files, which can be tested, reviewed, and deployed using automated pipelines. This enables teams to make changes quickly and confidently, knowing that changes are applied consistently across environments. Furthermore, IaC promotes the use of declarative configuration languages, such as YAML or JSON, which describe the desired state of infrastructure resources rather than the step-by-step instructions for provisioning them. This declarative approach simplifies infrastructure management and reduces the risk of configuration drift, where the actual state of infrastructure diverges from the desired state over time. As a result, teams can ensure that infrastructure configurations are always aligned with desired state, reducing the likelihood of deployment failures or inconsistencies. Popular tools and frameworks for implementing IaC include Terraform, AWS CloudFormation, Azure Resource Manager (ARM) templates, and Google Cloud Deployment Manager. These tools provide capabilities for defining *infrastructure resources, managing dependencies, and orchestrating deployment workflows. For example, Terraform is an open-source tool that allows users to define infrastructure resources in code using HashiCorp Configuration Language (HCL) and provision them across various cloud providers and on-premises environments. To use Terraform, teams write Terraform configuration files (.tf files) that define the desired state of infrastructure resources, including their type, properties, and dependencies. Once the configuration files are defined, teams use the Terraform CLI to initialize the project, plan changes, and apply configurations to create or update infrastructure resources. Similarly, AWS CloudFormation is a service provided by Amazon Web Services (AWS) that allows users to define infrastructure resources using JSON or YAML templates and provision them in a predictable and repeatable manner. Teams create CloudFormation templates that describe the desired state of infrastructure resources, such as EC2 instances, S3 buckets, and IAM roles, and use the CloudFormation CLI or AWS Management Console to deploy the templates and provision the resources. Azure Resource Manager (ARM) templates serve a similar purpose in the Microsoft Azure ecosystem, allowing users to define infrastructure resources using JSON templates and deploy them across Azure regions and subscriptions. Google Cloud Deployment*

Manager provides similar functionality for provisioning and managing infrastructure resources on Google Cloud Platform (GCP), using YAML or Jinja2 templates to define infrastructure configurations. Overall, IaC is a powerful practice that transforms infrastructure management and provisioning, enabling teams to define, deploy, and manage infrastructure resources using code and automation. By adopting IaC, teams can improve consistency, reliability, and efficiency in managing infrastructure, accelerate the deployment process, and deliver high-quality software products more effectively and reliably.

Integrating Infrastructure as Code (IaC) with Continuous Deployment (CD) pipelines is a crucial step in modern software development workflows. This integration streamlines the deployment process by automating the provisioning and management of infrastructure resources alongside application code deployments. By combining IaC with CD pipelines, teams can ensure consistency, reliability, and scalability in deploying both application code and infrastructure configurations. One of the primary benefits of integrating IaC with CD pipelines is the ability to define infrastructure resources as code and manage them alongside application code within version control repositories. This enables teams to track changes, review code, and collaborate on infrastructure configurations using the same processes and tools as application code. Additionally, integrating IaC with CD pipelines facilitates the automation of infrastructure provisioning and deployment, reducing manual effort and minimizing the risk of human error. Teams can use CI/CD tools such as Jenkins, Azure DevOps, GitLab CI/CD, or CircleCI to automate the deployment of infrastructure configurations alongside application code. For example, in Azure DevOps, teams can define IaC templates using Azure Resource Manager (ARM) templates or Terraform configuration files and include them in the same repository as their application code. Teams can then create CI/CD pipelines in Azure DevOps to build, test, and deploy both application code and infrastructure configurations in a coordinated manner. To deploy infrastructure configurations using Azure DevOps pipelines, teams can use tasks or steps to execute CLI commands or IaC tools, such as Terraform or Azure CLI, to provision and manage infrastructure resources. For instance, teams can use the Terraform CLI to apply Terraform configurations stored in a Git repository, which defines the desired state of infrastructure resources, such as virtual machines, networks, and storage accounts. By executing Terraform commands within Azure DevOps pipelines, teams can automate the deployment of infrastructure resources across Azure environments, ensuring consistency and repeatability in infrastructure deployments. Similarly, teams can use the Azure CLI within Azure DevOps pipelines to deploy Azure Resource Manager (ARM) templates, which describe the desired state of Azure resources using JSON or YAML syntax. The Azure CLI provides commands to validate, deploy, and manage ARM templates, enabling teams to automate the provisioning of Azure resources as part of their CD pipelines. Integrating IaC with CD pipelines also enables teams to implement infrastructure changes incrementally and safely. By defining infrastructure configurations as code, teams can version infrastructure changes, review them through code review processes, and deploy them using automated pipelines, reducing the risk of deployment failures or inconsistencies. Additionally, teams can leverage features such as rolling updates, canary deployments, or blue-green deployments to deploy infrastructure changes gradually and validate them in production environments before fully rolling them out. This approach allows teams to mitigate risks and ensure the reliability and stability of production environments during infrastructure deployments. Another benefit of integrating IaC with CD pipelines is the ability to manage infrastructure drift effectively. Infrastructure drift occurs when the actual state of infrastructure resources diverges from the desired state defined in code, due to manual changes or configuration drift *over time. By automating the deployment of infrastructure configurations using CD pipelines, teams can detect and remediate infrastructure drift automatically, ensuring that infrastructure resources remain aligned with desired state and reducing the likelihood of deployment failures or inconsistencies. Overall, integrating IaC with CD pipelines enables teams to automate the provisioning, deployment, and management of infrastructure resources alongside application code, ensuring consistency, reliability, and scalability in deploying software applications. By adopting this approach, teams can accelerate the delivery of software products, improve collaboration between development and operations teams, and deliver value to customers more efficiently and reliably.*

Chapter 10: Optimizing CD Pipelines for Efficiency and Reliability

Performance optimization techniques are essential for ensuring that software applications meet their performance requirements and deliver a satisfactory user experience. These techniques encompass various strategies and practices aimed at improving the speed, responsiveness, and efficiency of applications across different layers of the technology stack. One common performance optimization technique is code optimization, which involves identifying and eliminating bottlenecks, inefficiencies, and resource-intensive operations in application code. This may include optimizing algorithms, reducing the complexity of code, and minimizing unnecessary computations or memory allocations. Code optimization can significantly improve application performance and responsiveness, particularly in compute-intensive or latency-sensitive workloads. Another important aspect of performance optimization is database optimization, which focuses on improving the efficiency and scalability of database operations. This may involve optimizing SQL queries, creating appropriate indexes, partitioning data, and caching query results to reduce database latency and improve throughput. By optimizing database performance, teams can ensure that applications can handle increasing volumes of data and user traffic without experiencing performance degradation. In addition to code and database optimization, performance optimization techniques also encompass optimizing network and I/O operations. This may involve minimizing network latency by using content delivery networks (CDNs), optimizing data transfer protocols, and reducing the number of network round-trips required for communication between client and server. Similarly, optimizing I/O operations involves minimizing disk I/O, reducing file access times, and optimizing data serialization and deserialization to improve overall application performance. Performance optimization also extends to infrastructure optimization, which involves optimizing the underlying infrastructure resources, such as virtual machines, containers, and cloud services, to improve application performance and scalability. This may include optimizing resource allocation, scaling resources dynamically based on demand, and leveraging auto-scaling capabilities provided by cloud providers to handle fluctuations in workload. For example, teams can use CLI commands or infrastructure as code (IaC) tools such as Terraform or AWS CloudFormation to automate the provisioning and scaling of infrastructure resources based on predefined metrics or thresholds. Another important aspect of performance optimization is caching, which involves storing frequently accessed data or computed results in memory or fast storage to reduce latency and improve application responsiveness. This may include caching database query results, caching web page contents, or caching computed data to avoid redundant computations. By leveraging caching techniques, teams can reduce the load on backend systems, minimize response times, and improve overall application performance. Performance optimization also involves profiling and monitoring applications to identify performance bottlenecks and areas for improvement. This may include using profiling tools to analyze application performance metrics, such as CPU usage, memory usage, and response times, and identifying areas of code or functionality that contribute most to performance degradation. Teams can then prioritize optimization efforts based on profiling data and monitor application performance over time to ensure that performance improvements are effective and sustainable. Continuous performance testing is another critical aspect of performance optimization, which involves regularly testing application performance under various conditions and workloads to identify performance regressions and ensure that performance goals are met. This may include conducting load testing, stress testing, and endurance testing to evaluate how applications perform under different levels of concurrency, traffic, and resource usage. By incorporating performance testing into CI/CD pipelines, teams can detect performance issues early in the development lifecycle, iterate on performance improvements, and ensure that applications meet performance requirements before deployment to production environments. Overall, performance optimization is a multifaceted discipline that encompasses various strategies, practices, and techniques aimed at improving application performance and scalability. By applying code optimization, database optimization, network optimization, infrastructure optimization, caching, profiling, monitoring, and continuous performance testing, teams can ensure that applications deliver a fast, responsive, and reliable user experience, even under high loads and demanding conditions.

Reliability considerations play a crucial role in the design and implementation of Continuous Deployment (CD) pipelines, ensuring that software deployments are stable, predictable, and error-free. Reliability encompasses various aspects, including fault tolerance, error handling, rollback strategies, and monitoring, aimed at minimizing the impact of failures and disruptions on the application and its users. One key aspect of reliability in CD pipelines is fault tolerance, which involves designing systems and processes to withstand and recover from failures gracefully. This may include implementing redundancy, failover mechanisms, and error recovery strategies to ensure that deployments can continue uninterrupted in the event of infrastructure or service failures. By designing CD pipelines with fault tolerance in mind, teams can minimize downtime and ensure the reliability of deployments even in the face of unexpected failures. Error handling is another critical consideration in CD pipelines, as errors and failures can occur at any stage of the deployment process. This may include errors in code compilation, test failures, infrastructure provisioning errors, or deployment failures due to environmental inconsistencies. To handle errors effectively, teams can implement robust error handling mechanisms, such as retry logic, error logging, and automated notifications, to detect, diagnose, and resolve errors quickly and efficiently. By implementing effective error handling, teams can reduce the likelihood of deployment failures and minimize the impact of errors on the application and its users. Rollback strategies are essential for ensuring the reliability of deployments, enabling teams to revert to a stable state in case of deployment failures or issues. This may include implementing blue-green deployments, canary deployments, or feature toggles to enable gradual and controlled rollouts of changes, allowing teams to monitor deployments and roll back changes if issues are detected. By implementing rollback strategies, teams can minimize the impact of deployment failures, reduce downtime, and ensure the reliability of production environments. Monitoring is a critical aspect of reliability in CD pipelines, providing teams with visibility into the health, performance, and stability of deployments. This may include monitoring application metrics, infrastructure metrics, and deployment metrics using monitoring tools and platforms such as Prometheus, Grafana, Datadog, or New Relic. By monitoring deployments in real-time, teams can detect issues, anomalies, and performance degradations early, enabling them to respond proactively and mitigate risks before they impact users. Automated testing is another essential aspect of reliability in CD pipelines, enabling teams to validate changes, identify regressions, and ensure that deployments meet quality and reliability standards. This may include implementing automated unit tests, integration tests, regression tests, and end-to-end tests as part of the deployment process to verify the correctness and stability of changes. By automating testing, teams can reduce the risk of human error, accelerate the testing process, and ensure the reliability of deployments across different environments.

Configuration management is crucial for ensuring the consistency and reliability of deployments, enabling teams to manage and version infrastructure configurations, application configurations, and dependencies effectively. This may include using configuration management tools such as Ansible, Puppet, Chef, or SaltStack to automate the provisioning, configuration, and management of infrastructure resources and software components. By managing configurations as code, teams can ensure that deployments are consistent, reproducible, and reliable across different environments. Continuous validation is essential for ensuring the ongoing reliability of CD pipelines, enabling teams to validate changes, configurations, and deployments continuously. This may include implementing continuous validation checks, automated health checks, and synthetic monitoring to monitor the health and stability of deployments in real-time. By continuously validating deployments, teams can detect and resolve issues quickly, prevent outages, and ensure the reliability of production environments. Change management is a critical aspect of reliability in CD pipelines, enabling teams to manage and track changes to infrastructure, code, and configurations effectively. This may include implementing change management processes, version control systems, and release management practices to ensure that changes are reviewed, tested, and deployed in a controlled and systematic manner. By managing changes effectively, teams can minimize the risk of deployment failures, prevent configuration drift, and ensure the reliability and stability of production environments. In summary, reliability considerations are essential for designing and implementing robust and resilient CD pipelines. By focusing on fault tolerance, error handling, rollback strategies, monitoring, automated testing, configuration management, continuous validation, and change management, teams can ensure the reliability of deployments and deliver high-quality software products that meet the needs and expectations of users.

BOOK 3
ADVANCED AZURE DEVOPS TECHNIQUES
ARCHITECTING FOR SCALABILITY AND RESILIENCE -
EXAM AZ-400

ROB BOTWRIGHT

Chapter 1: Scalability Fundamentals in Azure DevOps

Understanding scalability in software systems is essential for building applications that can handle growing workloads and user demands effectively. Scalability refers to the ability of a system to handle increased load or demand by adding resources or scaling components horizontally or vertically. Horizontal scalability involves adding more instances of existing components, such as adding more servers or instances of a service, to distribute workload and accommodate increased traffic. Vertical scalability involves increasing the capacity of existing components, such as upgrading hardware resources like CPU, memory, or storage, to handle additional load or processing requirements. Scalability is crucial for ensuring that applications can accommodate growth without sacrificing performance, reliability, or user experience. One common approach to achieving scalability is through distributed architectures, which involve breaking down applications into smaller, independent components that can be deployed and scaled independently. This may include microservices architectures, where applications are composed of loosely coupled, independently deployable services that communicate via APIs or message queues. By decoupling components and distributing workload across multiple services, teams can scale individual components as needed, enabling applications to handle varying levels of load and traffic. Another approach to scalability is through the use of cloud computing platforms, which provide on-demand access to scalable computing resources, such as virtual machines, containers, and managed services. Cloud platforms such as Amazon Web Services (AWS), Microsoft Azure, and Google Cloud Platform (GCP) offer auto-scaling capabilities that enable teams to automatically scale resources based on demand, reducing the need for manual intervention and optimizing resource utilization. For example, teams can use AWS Auto Scaling groups or Azure Virtual Machine Scale Sets to automatically add or remove instances based on predefined scaling policies, such as CPU utilization or request rate. Scalability is not just about adding more resources or scaling components; it also involves designing applications and architectures to handle load and traffic efficiently. This may include optimizing algorithms, data structures, and caching strategies to reduce computational overhead and improve performance. By optimizing application code and architecture, teams can maximize resource utilization and minimize the impact of scaling on *application performance. Load balancing is another important aspect of scalability, enabling teams to distribute incoming traffic across multiple instances or servers to prevent overload and ensure optimal resource utilization. This may include using load balancers such as AWS Elastic Load Balancing, Azure Load Balancer, or NGINX to distribute incoming requests based on predefined algorithms, such as round-robin, least connections, or weighted distribution. By distributing workload across multiple instances, load balancers can help improve application availability, reliability, and scalability. Scaling databases is another critical consideration for achieving scalability in software systems, as databases often become a bottleneck as applications grow. This may include using techniques such as database sharding, replication, or partitioning to distribute data across multiple nodes or clusters, enabling databases to handle increased read and write throughput. For example, teams can use AWS RDS Read Replicas or Azure SQL Database Hyperscale to replicate database instances and distribute read queries across multiple replicas, improving read scalability and reducing latency. Additionally, teams can use techniques such as caching, denormalization, or indexing to optimize database performance and reduce the need for expensive queries or data access patterns. Monitoring and performance testing are essential for ensuring that applications can scale effectively and handle increased load or traffic. This may include monitoring key performance metrics, such as CPU utilization, memory usage, response times, and error rates, to identify performance bottlenecks and scalability issues. By monitoring performance metrics in real-time, teams can detect issues early, optimize resource allocation, and scale components as needed to maintain performance and reliability. Performance testing involves simulating realistic workloads and traffic patterns to evaluate application performance under different conditions and scalability scenarios. This may include conducting load testing, stress testing, and endurance testing to assess how applications perform under varying levels of concurrency, traffic, and resource usage. By identifying performance bottlenecks and scalability limitations through testing, teams can optimize application performance, scale resources effectively, and ensure that applications can handle growing workloads and user demands. In summary, scalability is a fundamental aspect of designing and building software systems that can grow and adapt to changing requirements and user demands. By leveraging distributed architectures, cloud computing platforms, optimization techniques, load balancing, database scaling, monitoring, and performance testing, teams can achieve scalability* and deliver high-performance, reliable applications that meet the needs of users and stakeholders. Key metrics for measuring scalability are essential for evaluating the performance, capacity, and efficiency of software systems as they grow and evolve. These metrics provide valuable insights into how well a system can handle increased workload, user traffic, and resource demands, enabling teams to identify scalability bottlenecks, optimize performance, and ensure the reliability and availability of applications. One key metric for measuring scalability is response time, which refers to the time taken for a system to respond to a user request or action. Response time is a critical indicator of system performance and user experience, as it directly impacts the perceived speed and responsiveness of applications. By monitoring response time under varying levels of load and traffic, teams can assess how well a system scales and identify performance bottlenecks that may affect user experience. Another important metric for measuring scalability is throughput, which refers to the number of requests or transactions processed by a system within a given time period. Throughput is a measure of system capacity and efficiency, indicating how well a system can handle concurrent requests or transactions without experiencing performance degradation or resource contention. By monitoring throughput metrics, teams can assess how well a system scales under increasing workload and identify resource constraints or bottlenecks that may limit scalability. Error rate is another critical metric for measuring scalability, as it indicates the reliability and robustness of a system under varying conditions. Error rate measures the percentage of failed requests or transactions relative to total requests, providing insights into the stability and resilience of applications. By monitoring error rate metrics, teams can identify scalability issues, such as service failures, timeouts, or resource exhaustion, and take proactive measures to mitigate risks and improve system reliability. Scalability metrics also include resource utilization, which refers to the amount of computational, memory, storage, or network resources consumed by a system under different levels of load and traffic. Resource utilization metrics provide insights into how efficiently a system utilizes available resources and how well it scales as workload increases. By monitoring resource utilization metrics, teams can identify resource bottlenecks, optimize resource allocation, and ensure that systems can handle growing demands without resource exhaustion or contention. Another important scalability metric is scalability ratio, which measures the ability of a system to maintain consistent performance and efficiency as workload increases. Scalability ratio *compares system performance or throughput under different levels of load or concurrency, indicating how well a system scales relative to its capacity. By calculating scalability ratios, teams can assess the scalability characteristics of a system and identify potential limitations or constraints that may affect scalability. Scalability metrics also include latency, which refers to the delay or time taken for a system to process a request or transaction. Latency metrics measure the responsiveness and efficiency of a system, indicating how quickly it can process requests and return results to users. By monitoring latency metrics, teams can assess the impact of increased workload on system performance and identify latency bottlenecks that may affect user experience. Another important scalability metric is fault tolerance, which measures the ability of a system to maintain availability and reliability in the face of failures or disruptions. Fault tolerance metrics include measures such as mean time to failure (MTTF), mean time to recovery (MTTR), and availability percentage, indicating how well a system handles failures and recovers from them. By monitoring fault tolerance metrics, teams can assess the resilience and robustness of a system and identify areas for improvement to ensure high availability and reliability. Scalability metrics also include cost-effectiveness, which measures the efficiency and affordability of scaling resources to meet growing demands. Cost-effectiveness metrics include measures such as cost per transaction, cost per user, or cost per throughput, indicating how efficiently resources are utilized and how well costs scale as workload increases. By monitoring cost-effectiveness metrics, teams can optimize resource allocation, minimize operational costs, and ensure that scaling strategies are cost-effective and sustainable. In summary, key metrics for measuring scalability provide valuable insights into the performance, capacity, reliability, and efficiency of software systems as they grow and evolve. By monitoring scalability metrics, teams can identify scalability bottlenecks, optimize performance, ensure reliability, and deliver high-quality applications that meet the needs of users and stakeholders.*

Chapter 2: Architectural Patterns for Scalable DevOps Solutions

Architectural patterns for scalability are essential for designing software systems that can handle growing workloads and user demands effectively. One common architectural pattern for scalability is the microservices architecture, which involves breaking down applications into smaller, loosely coupled services that can be developed, deployed, and scaled independently. Microservices architecture promotes modularity, flexibility, and scalability by decoupling components and enabling teams to scale individual services based on demand. Another common architectural pattern for scalability is the serverless architecture, which involves outsourcing infrastructure management to cloud providers and focusing on building event-driven, stateless functions that can scale automatically. Serverless architecture eliminates the need for managing servers and infrastructure, enabling teams to focus on building and deploying code without worrying about scalability or resource provisioning. Containerization is another architectural pattern for scalability, which involves packaging applications and dependencies into lightweight, portable containers that can be deployed consistently across different environments. Containers provide isolation, flexibility, and scalability by encapsulating applications and their dependencies, enabling teams to scale applications quickly and efficiently using container orchestration platforms such as Kubernetes or Docker Swarm. Another common architectural pattern for scalability is the event-driven architecture, which involves building applications around event-driven workflows and message passing. Event-driven architecture promotes scalability, responsiveness, and flexibility by decoupling components and enabling asynchronous communication between services. By using event-driven architecture, teams can scale components independently and handle varying levels of load and traffic efficiently. The layered architecture is another architectural pattern for scalability, which involves organizing applications into layers, such as presentation, business logic, and data access, to promote separation of concerns and scalability. Layered architecture enables teams to scale individual layers independently, allowing for more granular control over resource allocation and scalability. The distributed architecture is another architectural pattern for scalability, which involves distributing workload and processing across multiple nodes or servers to improve performance and scalability. Distributed architecture promotes fault tolerance, reliability, and scalability by distributing workload and processing across multiple nodes or servers, enabling applications to handle increased load and traffic effectively. Another common architectural pattern for scalability is the caching architecture, which involves using caching mechanisms to store frequently accessed data and improve performance and scalability. Caching architecture promotes scalability by reducing the need to access backend systems for data retrieval, enabling applications to respond to requests more quickly and efficiently. By using caching architecture, teams can improve application performance, reduce latency, and scale applications more effectively. The message queue architecture is another architectural pattern for scalability, which involves using message queues to decouple components and enable asynchronous communication between services. Message queue architecture promotes scalability by allowing components to process messages independently and handle varying levels of load and traffic efficiently. By using message queue architecture, teams can improve application responsiveness, reliability, and scalability. The shared-nothing architecture is another architectural pattern for scalability, which involves partitioning workload and data across multiple nodes or servers to improve performance and scalability. Shared-nothing architecture promotes scalability by distributing workload and data across multiple nodes or servers, enabling applications to handle increased load and traffic effectively. By using shared-nothing architecture, teams can improve application performance, reliability, and scalability. In summary, common architectural patterns for scalability provide valuable guidelines and best practices for designing and building software systems that can handle growing workloads and user demands effectively. By leveraging architectural patterns such as microservices, serverless, containerization, event-driven, layered, distributed, caching, message queue, and shared-nothing architecture, teams can design scalable, responsive, and reliable applications that meet the needs of users and stakeholders.

Choosing the right architecture for your DevOps solution is a crucial decision that can significantly impact the scalability, reliability, and efficiency of your software development and delivery process. The architecture you choose will determine how your DevOps tools and processes are implemented, integrated, and scaled to meet the needs of your organization and projects. One important consideration when choosing the architecture for your DevOps solution is the nature of your applications and workloads. Different architectures are better suited for different types of applications and workloads, so it's essential to assess your requirements and objectives carefully. For example, if you're building a microservices-based application with complex dependencies and interactions between services, a microservices architecture may be a suitable choice. Microservices architecture promotes modularity, flexibility, and scalability by breaking down applications into smaller, independently deployable services that can be developed, tested, and scaled independently. On the other hand, if you're building a simple, monolithic application with a straightforward architecture and minimal dependencies, a monolithic architecture may be a more straightforward and cost-effective choice. Monolithic architecture consolidates all application functionality into a single codebase and deployment unit, simplifying development, testing, and deployment processes. However, monolithic architecture may not be as flexible or scalable as microservices architecture, particularly for large, complex applications with diverse functionality and scalability requirements. Another consideration when choosing the architecture for your DevOps solution is the scalability and resource requirements of your applications and workloads. Scalability is essential for ensuring that your applications can handle increased load and traffic as they grow and evolve. Different architectures offer different scalability characteristics, so it's crucial to assess your scalability requirements and choose an architecture that can meet your needs. For example, if you anticipate significant fluctuations in workload or traffic, a scalable, distributed architecture may be a better choice than a monolithic architecture. Distributed architectures, such as microservices or serverless architectures, enable you to scale individual components or services independently, allowing you to allocate resources dynamically based on demand. Conversely, if your workload is relatively stable and predictable, a monolithic architecture may be sufficient, as it allows you to scale resources vertically by adding more powerful hardware or infrastructure. Security is another critical consideration when choosing the architecture for your DevOps solution. Security is essential for protecting your applications, data, and infrastructure from unauthorized access, breaches, and attacks. Different architectures offer different security features and capabilities, so it's essential to assess your security requirements and choose an architecture that can meet your needs. For example, if you're building a highly secure application that handles sensitive data or transactions, a microservices architecture with strong authentication, authorization, and encryption capabilities may be necessary. Microservices architecture allows you to implement security controls at the service level, enabling you to enforce security policies and access controls consistently across all services. Conversely, if security is less of a concern or if you're building a simple, internal application with minimal security requirements, a monolithic architecture may be sufficient. However, it's essential to ensure that your monolithic architecture follows security best practices and guidelines to mitigate potential risks and vulnerabilities. Another consideration when choosing the architecture for your DevOps solution is the complexity and maintainability of your applications and infrastructure. Different architectures offer different levels of complexity and maintainability, so it's essential to assess your capabilities and resources carefully. For example, if you have a small, inexperienced team with limited resources and expertise, a monolithic architecture may be a more manageable and maintainable choice. Monolithic architecture consolidates all application functionality into a single codebase and deployment unit, making it easier to develop, test, and deploy applications. Additionally, monolithic architecture may require less infrastructure and operational overhead, as you only need to manage a single deployment unit and environment. Conversely, if you have a large, experienced team with diverse skills and expertise, a more complex, distributed architecture may be feasible. Distributed architectures, such as microservices or serverless architectures, offer greater flexibility, scalability, *and resilience but may require more sophisticated tooling, processes, and practices to develop, deploy, and maintain effectively. Ultimately, choosing the right architecture for your DevOps solution requires careful consideration of your requirements, objectives, capabilities, and constraints. By assessing these factors and evaluating the pros and cons of different architectures, you can make an informed decision that aligns with your organization's goals and priorities. Additionally, it's essential to stay flexible and adaptable, as your requirements and circumstances may change over time, necessitating adjustments to your architecture and DevOps practices.*

Chapter 3: Leveraging Azure Services for Scalability

In the realm of cloud computing, Azure offers a wide array of scalable services designed to accommodate varying workloads and application demands. One of the most prominent services for scalability on Azure is Azure Virtual Machines (VMs), which provide flexible and scalable compute resources in the cloud. With Azure VMs, users can provision virtual machines of different sizes and configurations based on their specific requirements, allowing them to scale compute resources up or down as needed. To deploy a virtual machine on Azure using the CLI, you can use commands such as az vm create to create a new VM instance with specified configurations like size, image, and resource group. Another scalable service offered by Azure is Azure App Service, which provides a platform for building, deploying, and scaling web applications and APIs. With Azure App Service, users can deploy applications using various programming languages and frameworks, including .NET, Java, Node.js, Python, and PHP, and take advantage of features like automatic scaling and load balancing to handle varying levels of traffic. Using the CLI, you can deploy an Azure App Service using commands such as az webapp create to create a new web application instance, specifying configurations like the app name, resource group, and runtime stack. Azure Functions is another scalable service provided by Azure, offering a serverless computing platform for building and deploying event-driven, scalable applications and microservices. With Azure Functions, users can write and deploy functions that execute in response to triggers such as HTTP requests, message queue events, database changes, or timer events, allowing them to scale applications automatically based on demand. To deploy Azure Functions using the CLI, you can use commands such as az functionapp create to create a new function app instance and az functionapp deployment source config to configure deployment options like source control integration. Azure Kubernetes Service (AKS) is a managed Kubernetes service provided by Azure, offering a scalable, containerized orchestration platform for deploying, managing, and scaling containerized applications and microservices. With AKS, users can deploy and scale Kubernetes clusters in the cloud, allowing them to run containerized workloads efficiently and scale resources dynamically based on demand. To deploy an AKS cluster using the CLI, you can use commands such as az aks create to create a new Kubernetes cluster, specifying configurations like the node count, VM size, and Kubernetes version. Azure SQL Database is a scalable relational database service provided by Azure, offering fully managed, scalable database instances for running SQL Server workloads in the cloud. With Azure SQL Database, users can deploy and scale database instances based on their specific performance and storage requirements, allowing them to handle increasing data volumes and workload demands effectively. To deploy an Azure SQL Database using the CLI, you can use commands such as az sql server create to create a new SQL Server instance and az sql db create to create a new database within the server instance. Azure Cosmos DB is a globally distributed, multi-model database service provided by Azure, offering scalable and high-performance NoSQL databases for building globally distributed applications. With Azure Cosmos DB, users can deploy and scale databases with millisecond latency and guaranteed throughput, allowing them to handle massive workloads and scale resources dynamically based on demand. To deploy an Azure Cosmos DB using the CLI, you can use commands such as az cosmosdb create to create a new Cosmos DB account and az cosmosdb database create to create a new database within the account. Azure Blob Storage is a scalable object storage service provided by Azure, offering highly available and durable storage for storing large amounts of unstructured data, such as documents, images, videos, and logs. With Azure Blob Storage, users can store and scale data in the cloud, leveraging *features like geo-replication and lifecycle management to ensure data availability, durability, and accessibility. To deploy Azure Blob Storage using the CLI, you can use commands such as az storage account create to create a new storage account and az storage container create to create a new container within the account. Azure Cache for Redis is a scalable, distributed caching service provided by Azure, offering in-memory caching solutions for improving application performance and scalability. With Azure Cache for Redis, users can deploy and scale Redis caches in the cloud, enabling them to cache data, session state, and objects and reduce latency and database load. To deploy Azure Cache for Redis using the CLI, you can use commands such as az redis create to create a new Redis cache instance and az redis firewall-rule create to configure firewall rules for the cache instance. In summary, Azure offers a comprehensive suite of scalable services designed to meet the needs of modern applications and workloads. From virtual machines and web applications to serverless functions and containerized workloads, Azure provides a range of scalable solutions for building, deploying, and managing applications in the cloud. With its flexible and robust infrastructure, Azure enables users to scale resources dynamically based on demand, ensuring high performance, availability, and scalability for their applications and services.*

Integrating Azure services into DevOps pipelines is a critical aspect of modern software development and deployment, enabling teams to automate processes, streamline workflows, and improve collaboration across development, operations, and other stakeholders. One of the primary goals of integrating Azure services into DevOps pipelines is to automate the deployment and management of infrastructure and applications, reducing manual effort and minimizing errors. Azure DevOps provides a range of tools and services for building, testing, deploying, and monitoring applications, making it easier to integrate Azure services into DevOps pipelines seamlessly. Using Azure CLI, developers can automate various tasks and operations related to Azure services, such as provisioning resources, configuring settings, deploying applications, and managing infrastructure. For example, to create a new Azure resource group using the CLI, developers can use the command az group create, specifying parameters like the resource group name and location. Similarly, to deploy an application to Azure App Service using the CLI, developers can use commands such as az webapp deployment source config to configure deployment settings and az webapp deployment source to deploy application code from a source repository. Azure Pipelines is another essential component of Azure DevOps, providing a flexible and customizable platform for building, testing, and deploying applications across different environments and platforms. With Azure Pipelines, teams can define build and release pipelines that automate the entire software delivery process, from source code management to production deployment. Using Azure Pipelines, developers can integrate various Azure services into their DevOps workflows, such as Azure Container Registry for storing and managing Docker images, Azure Key Vault for securely storing and accessing secrets and keys, and Azure Monitor for monitoring application performance and health. To integrate Azure Container Registry into an Azure Pipelines build or release pipeline, developers can use tasks such as Docker@2 to build Docker images, Container Registry to push images to Azure Container Registry, and Azure CLI to authenticate and interact with the registry using CLI commands. Similarly, to integrate Azure Key Vault into an Azure Pipelines pipeline, developers can use tasks such as Azure Key Vault to fetch secrets and keys from Key Vault and Azure CLI to authenticate and interact with Key Vault using CLI commands. Azure DevOps also provides built-in support for integrating with other Azure services and third-party tools through extensions and integrations. For example, developers can use Azure DevOps extensions like Azure Resource Manager (ARM) template deployment task to deploy Azure resources using ARM templates, Azure Function Apps task to deploy and manage Azure Functions, and Azure Kubernetes Service (AKS) task to deploy and manage Kubernetes clusters. Additionally, developers can leverage integrations with popular third-party tools and services such as GitHub, Jenkins, Slack, and Jira to streamline collaboration, automate workflows, and enhance productivity. By integrating Azure services into DevOps pipelines, teams can achieve faster time-to-market, higher quality releases, and greater agility in responding to changing business requirements and market demands. However, it's essential to design and implement integration solutions carefully, considering factors such as security, compliance, scalability, and maintainability. Moreover, teams should continuously monitor and optimize their DevOps pipelines to ensure optimal performance, reliability, and efficiency. In summary, integrating Azure services into DevOps pipelines is essential for modern software development and deployment, enabling teams to automate processes, improve collaboration, and accelerate delivery cycles. With Azure DevOps and Azure CLI, developers have powerful tools and capabilities at their disposal to streamline workflows, automate tasks, and deploy applications with confidence in Azure environments.

Chapter 4: Designing Highly Available Systems in Azure DevOps

High availability is a fundamental principle in modern computing, essential for ensuring that applications and services remain accessible and operational, even in the face of hardware failures, software errors, or other disruptions. At its core, high availability is about designing systems and architectures in a way that minimizes downtime and maximizes uptime, allowing users to access and use applications and services whenever they need them. Achieving high availability requires implementing redundancy, fault tolerance, and resilience mechanisms at various levels of the infrastructure and application stack. Redundancy involves duplicating critical components or resources in a system to ensure that if one component fails, another can seamlessly take its place, preventing downtime and maintaining service availability. For example, in a high-availability web application architecture, redundant web servers are deployed across multiple data centers or regions to ensure continuous availability and fault tolerance. Using the Azure CLI, developers can provision redundant resources in Azure, such as redundant virtual machines, load balancers, and storage accounts, to achieve high availability. Fault tolerance refers to a system's ability to continue operating correctly in the event of a failure or fault, without impacting overall system performance or user experience. Fault-tolerant systems are designed to detect, isolate, and recover from failures automatically, ensuring that service availability is maintained even when individual components or resources fail. Implementing fault tolerance requires using techniques such as replication, failover, and graceful degradation to handle failures gracefully and minimize their impact on service availability. In Azure, developers can leverage services like Azure Traffic Manager for global load balancing and failover, Azure Application Gateway for HTTP load balancing and SSL termination, and Azure Storage replication for data redundancy and disaster recovery. Resilience is the ability of a system to adapt to changing conditions, recover from disruptions quickly, and continue operating effectively under stress or adverse circumstances. Resilient systems are designed to withstand failures, attacks, and other disruptions without compromising service availability or performance, ensuring that users can access and use applications and services without interruption. Building resilient systems requires implementing proactive monitoring, automated recovery, and self-healing mechanisms that can detect and respond to *anomalies, failures, or incidents in real-time. Azure provides a range of services and features for building resilient applications and services, such as Azure Monitor for monitoring and logging, Azure Automation for automated remediation, and Azure Site Recovery for disaster recovery and business continuity planning. High availability is not just about technology; it's also about people, processes, and culture. Achieving high availability requires a holistic approach that involves aligning business objectives, defining clear service-level objectives (SLOs) and service-level agreements (SLAs), establishing robust incident management and response processes, and fostering a culture of continuous improvement and learning. By prioritizing high availability and resilience in their architectures, organizations can minimize the impact of downtime, reduce the risk of revenue loss, protect their brand reputation, and ultimately deliver better experiences for their customers and users. In summary, high availability is a critical principle in modern computing, essential for ensuring that applications and services remain accessible and operational, even in the face of failures or disruptions. Achieving high availability requires implementing redundancy, fault tolerance, and resilience mechanisms at various levels of the infrastructure and application stack, leveraging technologies like Azure and best practices in people,* processes, and culture. With the right approach and tools, organizations can build and maintain highly available and resilient systems that meet the needs of their users and business objectives. Designing highly available architectures in Azure DevOps is crucial for ensuring the reliability and resilience of applications and services deployed on the Azure cloud platform. High availability refers to the ability of a system to remain operational and accessible even in the face of failures or disruptions, minimizing downtime and ensuring continuous service delivery to users. When designing highly available architectures in Azure DevOps, developers and architects must consider various factors, including infrastructure redundancy, fault tolerance mechanisms, disaster recovery strategies, and proactive monitoring and alerting systems. Redundancy is a key principle in achieving high availability, involving the replication and distribution of critical components and resources across multiple data centers, regions, or availability zones to eliminate single points of failure and ensure continuous service availability. Azure provides a range of services and features for implementing redundancy in architectures, such as Azure Availability Zones, which offer physically separate data centers within a region with independent power, cooling, and networking, ensuring high availability and fault tolerance. Using the Azure CLI, developers can deploy resources across multiple availability zones by specifying the appropriate parameters and configurations in their deployment scripts or templates. Fault tolerance mechanisms are essential for ensuring that applications and services can continue operating correctly in the event of failures or faults, without impacting overall system performance or user experience. Azure DevOps allows developers to implement fault tolerance by leveraging services like Azure Traffic Manager for global load balancing and failover, Azure Application Gateway for HTTP load balancing and SSL termination, and Azure DNS for high-performance and scalable DNS hosting. Disaster recovery strategies are critical for ensuring business continuity and minimizing the impact of catastrophic events such as natural disasters, hardware failures, or cyber-attacks. Azure offers various disaster recovery solutions, such as Azure Site Recovery, which provides automated replication and failover capabilities for virtual machines, ensuring seamless failover and recovery in the event of a disaster. Using the Azure CLI, developers can configure and manage disaster recovery plans and policies, define replication schedules, and initiate failover operations to ensure business continuity and data protection. Proactive monitoring and alerting systems play a crucial role in identifying and mitigating potential issues before they escalate into *full-blown outages or disruptions. Azure Monitor is a comprehensive monitoring and diagnostics service provided by Azure, offering a unified platform for monitoring the performance, availability, and health of Azure resources and applications. Developers can use Azure Monitor to collect and analyze telemetry data, set up custom alerts and notifications, and gain insights into the overall health and performance of their Azure DevOps environments. Leveraging the Azure CLI, developers can configure monitoring settings, create custom metrics and alerts, and automate remediation actions based on predefined thresholds or conditions. When designing highly available architectures in Azure DevOps, it's essential to follow best practices and architectural patterns that promote scalability, reliability, and resilience. Some common architectural patterns for achieving high availability in Azure DevOps include active-active and active-passive architectures, which involve deploying redundant resources across multiple regions or data centers to ensure continuous service availability and fault tolerance. Additionally, developers should implement auto-scaling and load balancing mechanisms to handle fluctuations in demand and ensure optimal performance under varying workload conditions. Azure DevOps also provides built-in support for blue-green deployments, canary releases, and feature flags, allowing developers to roll out new features and updates gradually and mitigate risks associated with deployments. In summary, designing highly available architectures in Azure DevOps is essential for ensuring the reliability, resilience, and scalability of applications and services deployed on the Azure cloud platform. By leveraging redundancy, fault tolerance mechanisms, disaster recovery strategies, and proactive monitoring and alerting systems, developers can build resilient and robust architectures that meet the demands of modern cloud-native applications and ensure continuous service delivery to users. With the flexibility and scalability of Azure DevOps and the rich set of services and features provided by Azure, organizations can design and deploy highly available architectures that drive business growth and innovation.*

Chapter 5: Implementing Fault Tolerance and Disaster Recovery

Fault tolerance strategies in Azure DevOps are paramount for maintaining the reliability and resilience of applications and services deployed on the Azure cloud platform. Fault tolerance refers to a system's ability to continue operating correctly in the event of failures or faults, without compromising overall system performance or user experience. Implementing fault tolerance strategies in Azure DevOps involves designing architectures and workflows that can detect, isolate, and recover from failures automatically, ensuring continuous service availability and reliability. One key aspect of fault tolerance in Azure DevOps is redundancy, which involves duplicating critical components or resources in a system to eliminate single points of failure and ensure continuous service availability. Azure provides a range of services and features for implementing redundancy in architectures, such as Azure Availability Zones, which offer physically separate data centers within a region with independent power, cooling, and networking. Using the Azure CLI, developers can deploy resources across multiple availability zones to achieve fault tolerance by specifying the appropriate parameters and configurations in their deployment scripts or templates. Another essential aspect of fault tolerance in Azure DevOps is implementing automatic failover mechanisms, which enable applications and services to switch seamlessly to backup systems or resources in the event of failures or disruptions. Azure Traffic Manager is a global DNS-based traffic load balancer that enables automatic failover and failback between healthy endpoints in different regions or data centers. Developers can configure failover policies and settings using the Azure CLI to ensure continuous service availability and fault tolerance in Azure DevOps environments. Additionally, Azure provides built-in support for automatic scaling, which allows applications and services to dynamically adjust resource allocation based on demand to maintain optimal performance and availability under varying workload conditions. Azure Autoscale is a service that enables automatic scaling of Azure virtual machine scale sets, web apps, and other Azure resources based on predefined metrics and thresholds. Developers can use the Azure CLI to configure autoscaling policies and settings, define scaling rules, and monitor scaling activities in real-time to ensure fault tolerance and performance optimization in Azure DevOps environments. Implementing fault tolerance in Azure DevOps also requires proactive monitoring and alerting systems that can detect and respond to anomalies, failures, or incidents in real-time. Azure Monitor is a comprehensive monitoring and diagnostics service provided by Azure, offering a unified platform for monitoring the performance, availability, and health of Azure resources and applications. Developers can use Azure Monitor to collect and analyze telemetry data, set up custom alerts and notifications, and gain insights into the overall health and performance of their Azure DevOps environments. Leveraging the Azure CLI, developers can configure monitoring settings, create custom metrics and alerts, and automate remediation actions based on predefined thresholds or conditions to ensure fault tolerance and resilience in Azure DevOps environments. Disaster recovery strategies are another critical aspect of fault tolerance in Azure DevOps, ensuring business continuity and data protection in the event of catastrophic events such as natural disasters, hardware failures, or cyber-attacks. Azure Site Recovery is a disaster recovery service provided by Azure that enables automated replication, failover, and failback of virtual machines and workloads across different regions or data centers. Using the Azure CLI, developers can configure disaster recovery plans and policies, define replication schedules, and initiate failover operations to ensure continuous service availability and fault tolerance in Azure DevOps environments.

In summary, fault tolerance strategies are essential for maintaining the reliability and resilience of applications and services deployed on the Azure cloud platform. By implementing redundancy, automatic failover mechanisms, automatic scaling, proactive monitoring and alerting systems, and disaster recovery strategies, developers can ensure continuous service availability and reliability in Azure DevOps environments. With the flexibility and scalability of Azure and the rich set of services and features provided by Azure DevOps, organizations can design and deploy fault-tolerant architectures that meet the demands of modern cloud-native applications and ensure business continuity and data protection.

Disaster recovery planning and implementation are critical aspects of ensuring business continuity and data protection in the face of catastrophic events such as natural disasters, hardware failures, or cyber-attacks. Developing a comprehensive disaster recovery plan involves assessing potential risks and threats to business operations, identifying critical systems and data, and defining strategies and procedures for mitigating risks and minimizing downtime. In Azure DevOps, disaster recovery planning begins with understanding the different types of disasters that could impact your organization and the potential impact they could have on your operations. Once you have identified potential risks and threats, you can begin to assess the resilience of your existing infrastructure and applications and identify any vulnerabilities or single points of failure that need to be addressed. Using the Azure CLI, developers can assess the resilience of their Azure DevOps environments by running diagnostics commands to identify potential issues or weaknesses in their infrastructure or configurations. Once you have assessed the resilience of your Azure DevOps environment, you can begin to develop a disaster recovery plan that outlines the steps and procedures for responding to and recovering from different types of disasters. A disaster recovery plan should include detailed instructions for backing up critical data and applications, replicating data to off-site locations or backup regions, and restoring services and operations in the event of a disaster. Using the Azure CLI, developers can configure and manage backup and replication settings for Azure resources such as virtual machines, databases, and storage accounts to ensure data protection and availability in the event of a disaster. Additionally, developers can use Azure Site Recovery to automate the replication, failover, and failback of virtual machines and workloads across different regions or data centers, ensuring business continuity and data protection in the event of a disaster. Implementing a disaster recovery plan also involves testing and validating the plan to ensure that it is effective and reliable in real-world scenarios. Regularly testing your disaster recovery plan helps identify any gaps or weaknesses in your procedures and allows you to make any necessary adjustments or improvements before a real disaster occurs. Using the Azure CLI, developers can simulate disaster scenarios and test failover and recovery procedures by initiating failover operations, restoring backups, and verifying data integrity and availability. It's essential to involve key stakeholders from across the organization in the testing and validation process to ensure that everyone understands their roles and responsibilities and that the plan is aligned with business objectives and requirements. Once you have tested and validated your disaster recovery plan, it's crucial to document and communicate the plan to all relevant stakeholders and ensure that everyone knows what to do in the event of a disaster. Regular training and drills can help reinforce procedures and ensure that everyone is prepared to respond effectively in a crisis. In summary, disaster recovery planning and implementation are essential for ensuring business continuity and data protection in Azure DevOps environments. By assessing potential risks and threats, developing a comprehensive disaster recovery plan, and regularly testing and validating the plan, organizations can minimize downtime, mitigate risks, and ensure that critical systems and data are protected and available in the event of a disaster. With the flexibility and scalability of Azure and the rich set of services and features provided by Azure DevOps, organizations can design and deploy robust disaster recovery solutions that meet the demands of modern cloud-native applications and ensure business continuity and data protection.

Chapter 6: Scaling CI/CD Pipelines for Large Projects

Scaling Continuous Integration and Continuous Deployment (CI/CD) processes for large projects presents a myriad of challenges that organizations must navigate to maintain efficiency and reliability in their software delivery pipelines. One of the primary challenges lies in managing the complexity that arises as projects grow in size, encompassing multiple code repositories, numerous dependencies, and intricate interdependencies between various components. As the codebase expands, so too does the volume of code changes, leading to longer build times and increased strain on CI/CD infrastructure. To address these challenges, organizations must invest in scalable CI/CD architectures that can accommodate the growing demands of large projects. Leveraging cloud-based CI/CD solutions such as Azure DevOps can provide the scalability and flexibility needed to handle the complexities of large-scale software development projects. With Azure DevOps, organizations can dynamically allocate computing resources based on workload demands, ensuring that builds and deployments can scale to meet the needs of large projects. Using the Azure CLI, developers can automate the provisioning and configuration of CI/CD pipelines, enabling seamless scalability and resource management. Another challenge of scaling CI/CD for large projects is managing dependencies and ensuring consistency across different environments. As projects grow, so too does the number of dependencies that need to be managed, including libraries, frameworks, and third-party services. Ensuring that all dependencies are up-to-date and compatible with each other can be a daunting task, particularly in large, complex projects with numerous contributors. To address this challenge, organizations can implement dependency management strategies and tools that automate the process of tracking, updating, and resolving dependencies. Azure DevOps provides built-in support for dependency management, allowing organizations to define dependency versions and constraints, automate dependency resolution, and ensure consistency across different environments. By leveraging Azure DevOps artifact repositories, organizations can centralize dependency management and ensure that all team members have access to the latest versions of dependencies. Additionally, organizations can use Azure DevOps pipelines to automate the process of testing and validating dependencies, ensuring that changes to dependencies do not introduce regressions or compatibility issues. Another challenge of scaling CI/CD for large projects is managing the growing number of tests and test suites that need to be executed as part of the software delivery pipeline. As projects grow in size and complexity, so too does the number of tests that need to be run to ensure the quality and reliability of the software. Managing test execution times and optimizing test suites for efficiency becomes increasingly important as projects scale. To address this challenge, organizations can implement strategies and techniques for optimizing test execution times and reducing test suite complexity. This may include parallelizing test execution, prioritizing critical tests, and implementing techniques such as test data management and test isolation to streamline the testing process. With Azure DevOps, organizations can leverage built-in features such as parallel test execution and test scheduling to optimize test execution times and improve overall pipeline efficiency. By distributing test execution across multiple agents and environments, organizations can reduce build times and ensure that tests are completed in a timely manner. Additionally, organizations can use Azure DevOps analytics and reporting features to gain insights into test execution times and identify opportunities for optimization. Another challenge of scaling CI/CD for large projects is managing the growing number of environments and deployment targets that need to be supported. As projects grow, so too does the *complexity of the deployment landscape, encompassing multiple environments such as development, staging, and production, as well as various deployment targets such as on-premises servers, cloud platforms, and hybrid environments. Managing the configuration and provisioning of these environments can be challenging, particularly in large, distributed teams with diverse deployment requirements. To address this challenge, organizations can implement infrastructure as code (IaC) and configuration management techniques to automate the provisioning and management of environments and deployment targets. With tools such as Azure Resource Manager (ARM) templates and Terraform, organizations can define infrastructure configurations as code and automate the deployment and management of infrastructure resources. By treating infrastructure as code, organizations can ensure consistency and repeatability across different environments and deployment targets, reducing the risk of configuration drift and deployment errors. Additionally, organizations can use Azure DevOps release pipelines to automate the deployment process and orchestrate the release of software across different environments. By defining release pipelines as code, organizations can automate the deployment process and ensure that releases are consistent and reproducible across different environments. In summary, scaling CI/CD for large projects presents a range of challenges that organizations must address to maintain efficiency and reliability in their software delivery pipelines. By investing in scalable CI/CD architectures, implementing dependency management strategies, optimizing test execution times, and automating environment provisioning and deployment, organizations can overcome these challenges and ensure that their CI/CD processes can scale to meet the demands of large projects. With Azure DevOps and the rich set of features and capabilities provided by the Azure cloud platform, organizations can build and deploy software at scale with confidence, knowing that their CI/CD pipelines are robust, efficient, and reliable.*

Optimizing Continuous Integration/Continuous Deployment (CI/CD) pipelines for scale is essential to ensure efficient and reliable software delivery in modern development environments. One key strategy for optimizing CI/CD pipelines for scale is to adopt a microservices architecture, where applications are broken down into smaller, independent components that can be built, tested, and deployed separately. By breaking down monolithic applications into microservices, organizations can parallelize build and deployment processes, reduce build times, and improve overall pipeline efficiency. Using the Azure CLI, developers can automate the deployment of microservices-based applications by defining separate CI/CD pipelines for each microservice and orchestrating the deployment of microservices using containerization technologies such as Docker and Kubernetes. Another strategy for optimizing CI/CD pipelines for scale is to implement build caching and dependency management techniques to reduce build times and improve build performance. By caching dependencies and build artifacts, organizations can avoid redundant builds and minimize the time required to build and test applications. With Azure DevOps, developers can configure build pipelines to cache dependencies and build artifacts, ensuring that subsequent builds are faster and more efficient. Additionally, organizations can leverage distributed build systems and build agents to parallelize builds and distribute build workloads across multiple machines or environments. By spreading build workloads across multiple agents, organizations can reduce build times and improve overall pipeline throughput. Continuous integration (CI) and continuous deployment (CD) play crucial roles in modern software development practices. To optimize CI/CD pipelines for scale, organizations should adopt best practices such as modularizing codebases, implementing build caching, and leveraging distributed build systems. Modularizing codebases involves breaking down monolithic applications into smaller, independently deployable components, allowing teams to parallelize development efforts and scale CI/CD pipelines more effectively. By modularizing codebases, organizations can reduce build times, minimize dependencies between components, and improve overall pipeline performance. Additionally, organizations should implement build caching techniques to reduce build times and improve build performance. By caching dependencies, build artifacts, and intermediate build outputs, organizations can avoid redundant builds and minimize the time required to build and test applications. With Azure DevOps, developers can configure build pipelines to cache dependencies and build artifacts, ensuring that subsequent builds are faster and more efficient. Distributed build systems play a crucial role in optimizing CI/CD pipelines for scale. By distributing build workloads across multiple agents or environments, organizations can parallelize builds and increase pipeline throughput. With Azure DevOps, organizations can leverage distributed build systems to scale CI/CD pipelines effectively. By provisioning additional build agents and configuring build pipelines to distribute workloads across multiple agents, organizations can reduce build times and improve overall pipeline performance. Another *strategy for optimizing CI/CD pipelines for scale is to implement automated testing and validation processes. By automating the execution of tests and validation checks, organizations can ensure that code changes meet quality standards and are compatible with existing systems and dependencies. With Azure DevOps, organizations can configure build pipelines to automatically trigger tests and validation checks after each code commit, ensuring that code changes are thoroughly tested before being deployed to production. Additionally, organizations can leverage automated testing frameworks and tools to streamline the testing process and reduce the time required to identify and fix defects. By automating testing and validation processes, organizations can improve overall pipeline efficiency and reduce the risk of deploying faulty code to production. In summary, optimizing CI/CD pipelines for scale is essential for ensuring efficient and reliable software delivery in modern development environments. By adopting best practices such as modularizing codebases, implementing build caching, leveraging distributed build systems, and automating testing and validation processes, organizations can scale CI/CD pipelines effectively and accelerate the delivery of high-quality software products. With Azure DevOps and the rich set of features and capabilities provided by the Azure cloud platform, organizations can build* and deploy software at scale with confidence, knowing that their CI/CD pipelines are robust, efficient, and reliable.

Chapter 7: Performance Optimization Strategies in Azure DevOps

Identifying performance bottlenecks in Azure DevOps is crucial for ensuring the efficiency and reliability of software delivery pipelines. Performance bottlenecks can manifest in various areas of the CI/CD process, including build times, deployment speeds, and overall pipeline throughput. One common performance bottleneck in Azure DevOps is long build times, which can result from a variety of factors, including large codebases, complex build configurations, and resource limitations. To identify performance bottlenecks in build times, organizations can use the Azure CLI to monitor build metrics such as queue times, build durations, and resource utilization. By analyzing these metrics, organizations can pinpoint areas of inefficiency in their build processes and take steps to optimize performance. Another performance bottleneck in Azure DevOps is slow deployment speeds, which can delay the delivery of new features and updates to end users. Slow deployment speeds can be caused by factors such as large deployment packages, inefficient deployment scripts, and resource constraints. To identify performance bottlenecks in deployment speeds, organizations can use the Azure CLI to monitor deployment metrics such as deployment durations, success rates, and error rates. By analyzing these metrics, organizations can identify areas of inefficiency in their deployment processes and implement optimizations to improve performance. Additionally, organizations can leverage Azure DevOps features such as deployment slots and canary deployments to gradually roll out changes and minimize downtime during deployments. Another common performance bottleneck in Azure DevOps is limited pipeline throughput, which can result from factors such as inadequate build agent capacity, network congestion, and inefficient pipeline configurations. To identify performance bottlenecks in pipeline throughput, organizations can use the Azure CLI to monitor pipeline metrics such as queue lengths, pipeline durations, and resource utilization. By analyzing these metrics, organizations can identify areas of congestion and inefficiency in their pipelines and take steps to improve throughput. This may involve scaling up build agent capacity, optimizing network configurations, or redesigning pipeline workflows to reduce resource contention. Additionally, organizations can leverage Azure DevOps features such as parallel execution and dependency caching to optimize pipeline performance and improve throughput. In summary, identifying performance bottlenecks in Azure

DevOps is essential for maintaining the efficiency and reliability of software delivery pipelines. By using the Azure CLI to monitor build, deployment, and pipeline metrics, organizations can pinpoint areas of inefficiency and take steps to optimize performance. Whether it's optimizing build times, improving deployment speeds, or increasing pipeline throughput, organizations can leverage Azure DevOps and the rich set of features provided by the Azure cloud platform to streamline their CI/CD processes and deliver high-quality software products with confidence.

Performance optimization is a critical aspect of software development that aims to improve the speed, responsiveness, and efficiency of applications. One technique for performance optimization is code profiling, which involves analyzing the execution of code to identify performance bottlenecks and areas for improvement. Developers can use tools such as Visual Studio Profiler or JetBrains dotTrace to profile their code and identify hotspots that contribute to slow performance. By analyzing the results of code profiling, developers can optimize critical sections of code, such as loops or database queries, to improve overall application performance. Another technique for performance optimization is database indexing, which involves creating indexes on database tables to speed up query execution. Indexes allow database systems to quickly locate and retrieve data, reducing the time required to execute queries and improving overall application performance. Developers can use SQL commands such as CREATE INDEX to create indexes on database tables and columns that are frequently queried. By strategically indexing database tables, developers can optimize query performance and improve the responsiveness of applications that rely on database access. Additionally, developers can use caching techniques to improve application performance by storing frequently accessed data in memory for faster retrieval. By caching data at various layers of the application stack, such as the database, web server, or client browser, developers can reduce the time required to fetch data from disk or over the network. Techniques such as output caching, query caching, and session caching can be used to cache data at different levels of the application stack, depending on the nature of the data and its access patterns. By implementing caching strategies, developers can improve application responsiveness and reduce server load, leading to better overall performance. Another technique for performance optimization is code refactoring, which involves restructuring and rewriting code to improve readability, maintainability, and performance. Developers can use techniques such as method extraction, loop unrolling, and code consolidation to *simplify complex code and eliminate unnecessary overhead. By refactoring code to remove redundant calculations, reduce memory allocations, and minimize function calls, developers can improve application performance and reduce execution times. Additionally, developers can use performance monitoring and profiling tools to identify areas of code that can be optimized through refactoring. By continuously monitoring application performance and profiling code execution, developers can identify opportunities for refactoring and optimization that can lead to significant performance improvements. In summary, performance optimization is an essential aspect of software development that involves identifying and addressing performance bottlenecks to improve application speed, responsiveness, and efficiency. By employing techniques such as code profiling, database indexing, caching, and code refactoring, developers can optimize application performance and deliver high-quality software that meets the needs of users and stakeholders. With the right tools, techniques, and practices, developers can continuously improve application performance and provide users with fast, reliable, and responsive software experiences.*

Chapter 8: Security Best Practices for Scalable Architectures

Security considerations are paramount when designing and implementing scalable architectures, ensuring that systems remain protected against potential threats and vulnerabilities as they grow in size and complexity. One essential aspect of security in scalable architectures is identity and access management, which involves controlling user access to resources and ensuring that only authorized individuals can perform certain actions within the system. Organizations can use tools such as Azure Active Directory (AD) to manage user identities and enforce access controls across their environments. With Azure AD, administrators can define user roles, assign permissions, and implement multi-factor authentication to verify user identities and protect against unauthorized access. Additionally, organizations can use role-based access control (RBAC) to grant fine-grained permissions to users based on their roles and responsibilities within the organization. RBAC allows organizations to limit access to sensitive resources and data, reducing the risk of unauthorized access and data breaches. Another critical aspect of security in scalable architectures is network security, which involves protecting data as it moves between different components of the system and ensuring that communication channels remain secure and encrypted. Organizations can use virtual private networks (VPNs) and secure sockets layer (SSL) encryption to establish secure connections between components and prevent eavesdropping and tampering. Additionally, organizations can implement network segmentation and firewalls to isolate different parts of the system and prevent unauthorized access to sensitive resources. By securing communication channels and implementing network security best practices, organizations can protect data as it travels across the network and reduce the risk of interception and data theft. Data security is another important consideration in scalable architectures, involving protecting sensitive data from unauthorized access, disclosure, and modification. Organizations can use encryption techniques such as data encryption at rest and in transit to protect data stored in databases and transmitted between different components of the system. By encrypting data using strong cryptographic algorithms and keys, organizations can ensure that sensitive information remains secure, even if it falls into the wrong hands. Additionally, organizations can implement data masking and anonymization techniques to obfuscate sensitive information and prevent *unauthorized users from accessing or identifying personal or confidential data. By implementing data security best practices, organizations can protect sensitive information and comply with data protection regulations such as the General Data Protection Regulation (GDPR) and the Health Insurance Portability and Accountability Act (HIPAA). Security monitoring and incident response are essential components of security in scalable architectures, involving continuously monitoring system activity for signs of unauthorized access, suspicious behavior, or security breaches. Organizations can use tools such as Azure Security Center and Azure Monitor to monitor system activity, analyze security logs, and detect potential security incidents in real-time. Additionally, organizations can implement security information and event management (SIEM) systems to aggregate and correlate security events from different sources and generate alerts for suspicious activity. By monitoring system activity and responding promptly to security incidents, organizations can mitigate the impact of security breaches and prevent further damage to their systems and data. Compliance with industry regulations and standards is another important aspect of security in scalable architectures, involving ensuring that systems meet the requirements of relevant regulatory frameworks and industry* standards. *Organizations can use tools such as Azure Policy and Azure Compliance Manager to assess their compliance with regulations such as GDPR, HIPAA, and the Payment Card Industry Data Security Standard (PCI DSS). By implementing security controls and policies that align with regulatory requirements and industry standards, organizations can demonstrate their commitment to security and build trust with customers and stakeholders. In summary, security considerations are critical when designing and implementing scalable architectures, ensuring that systems remain protected against potential threats and vulnerabilities. By implementing identity and access management controls, network security measures, data encryption techniques, security monitoring and incident response processes, and compliance frameworks, organizations can build secure and resilient architectures that meet the needs of their users and stakeholders. With the right tools, techniques, and practices, organizations can protect sensitive information, mitigate security risks, and maintain the confidentiality, integrity, and availability of their systems and data. Implementing security controls in Azure DevOps is essential for safeguarding the integrity, confidentiality, and availability of software development pipelines and environments. One crucial aspect of implementing security controls is securing access to Azure DevOps resources, which involves controlling who can access the Azure DevOps organization, projects, repositories, and pipelines. Organizations can use Azure Active Directory (AD) to manage user identities and enforce access controls based on user roles and permissions. By integrating Azure DevOps with Azure AD, organizations can implement single sign-on (SSO) and enforce multi-factor authentication (MFA) to verify user identities and prevent unauthorized access. Additionally, organizations can use Azure DevOps RBAC (Role-Based Access Control) to assign granular permissions to users and groups, restricting access to sensitive resources and data. To configure RBAC in Azure DevOps, administrators can use the Azure CLI to define custom roles and assign permissions to users and groups. By carefully managing access controls, organizations can reduce the risk of unauthorized access and data breaches in Azure DevOps environments. Another critical aspect of implementing security controls in Azure DevOps is securing source code repositories, which contain valuable intellectual property and sensitive information. Organizations can use Git repositories in Azure DevOps to store and manage source code securely, leveraging features such as branch policies, code reviews, and branch permissions to control access and enforce code quality standards. To secure Git repositories in Azure DevOps, organizations can use branch policies to enforce requirements such as code reviews, work item linking, and build validation before code changes can be merged into the main branch. Additionally, organizations can use branch permissions to restrict access to specific branches and prevent unauthorized users from making changes to critical code bases. By implementing these security controls, organizations can prevent unauthorized access to source code repositories and maintain the integrity and confidentiality of their code bases. Another important aspect of implementing security controls in Azure DevOps is securing build and release pipelines, which automate the process of building, testing, and deploying software applications. Organizations can use Azure DevOps pipelines to define and execute CI/CD workflows, leveraging features such as gated builds, signed artifacts, and release gates to enforce security controls throughout the pipeline lifecycle. To secure build and release pipelines in Azure DevOps, organizations can use gated builds to require approval before changes can be merged into the main branch or deployed to production environments. Additionally, organizations can use signed artifacts to ensure that only trusted artifacts are deployed to production environments, reducing the risk of deploying malicious or tampered code. By implementing release gates, organizations can enforce additional security checks, such as vulnerability scanning and compliance checks, before deploying changes to production environments. By securing build and release pipelines in Azure DevOps, organizations can mitigate the risk of introducing vulnerabilities or deploying insecure code into production environments, reducing the likelihood of security incidents and data breaches. In summary, implementing security controls in Azure DevOps is essential for protecting software development pipelines and environments against potential threats and vulnerabilities. By securing access to Azure DevOps resources, securing source code repositories, and securing build and release pipelines, organizations can reduce the risk of unauthorized access, data breaches, and security incidents. With the right security controls in place, organizations can build and deploy software applications with confidence, knowing that their systems and data are protected against security threats.*

Chapter 9: Advanced Monitoring and Alerting for Resilient Systems

Implementing advanced monitoring solutions in Azure DevOps is essential for gaining insight into the performance, availability, and reliability of software applications and infrastructure. One crucial aspect of implementing advanced monitoring solutions is defining key performance indicators (KPIs) and metrics that provide actionable insights into the health and performance of applications and services. Organizations can use tools such as Azure Monitor to collect and analyze telemetry data from various sources, including application logs, performance counters, and infrastructure metrics. By defining KPIs such as response time, error rate, and resource utilization, organizations can monitor the performance of their applications and detect issues before they impact users. To configure Azure Monitor to collect telemetry data, organizations can use the Azure portal or the Azure CLI to enable monitoring for Azure resources and configure diagnostic settings for virtual machines, web applications, and other services. By collecting telemetry data from across the environment, organizations can gain a comprehensive view of their applications and infrastructure and identify areas for optimization and improvement. Another critical aspect of implementing advanced monitoring solutions is creating dashboards and visualizations that provide real-time visibility into the performance and health of applications and services. Organizations can use tools such as Azure Monitor Workbooks to create custom dashboards that aggregate and visualize telemetry data from multiple sources. By creating dashboards that display KPIs, trends, and anomalies, organizations can quickly identify performance issues and take corrective action to mitigate their impact. To create custom dashboards in Azure Monitor Workbooks, organizations can use the Azure portal or the Azure CLI to define queries and visualizations that display relevant metrics and data. By sharing dashboards with development teams, operations teams, and other stakeholders, organizations can foster collaboration and empower teams to proactively monitor and manage the health of their applications and services. Additionally, organizations can use alerts and notifications to proactively monitor for issues and respond to incidents in real-time. Azure Monitor allows organizations to create alert rules that trigger notifications when predefined conditions are met, such as when response time exceeds a certain threshold or when the error rate exceeds a specified percentage. To create alert rules in Azure Monitor, organizations can use the Azure portal or the Azure CLI to define alert conditions, thresholds, and notification channels. By configuring alert rules to notify relevant stakeholders, organizations can ensure that issues are promptly addressed and resolved, minimizing the impact on users and business operations. Furthermore, organizations can use advanced analytics and machine learning techniques to detect and diagnose issues in real-time. Azure Monitor offers features such as anomaly detection and log analytics that use machine learning algorithms to analyze telemetry data and identify patterns and anomalies indicative of potential issues. By leveraging these advanced analytics capabilities, organizations can detect issues early, predict future trends, and proactively address potential problems before they impact users. To enable anomaly detection and log analytics in Azure Monitor, organizations can use the Azure portal or the Azure CLI to configure data collection and define analysis queries. By harnessing the power of machine learning and advanced analytics, organizations can gain deeper insights into the performance and behavior of their applications and infrastructure, enabling them to optimize performance, enhance reliability, and improve the overall user experience. In summary, implementing advanced monitoring solutions in Azure DevOps is essential for gaining visibility, insight, and control over the performance and *health of software applications and infrastructure. By defining KPIs, creating dashboards and visualizations, configuring alerts and notifications, and leveraging advanced analytics and machine learning, organizations can monitor their applications and services proactively, detect issues early, and take timely corrective action to ensure optimal performance and reliability. With the right monitoring solutions in place, organizations can achieve greater operational efficiency, reduce downtime, and deliver a superior user experience. Configuring alerts for resilience and performance monitoring is crucial for maintaining the reliability and availability of software applications and infrastructure. Organizations rely on alerts to notify them of potential issues or abnormalities that may affect the performance or health of their systems. Azure Monitor provides a robust alerting mechanism that allows organizations to define custom alert rules based on specific conditions and thresholds. To configure alerts in Azure Monitor, organizations can use the Azure portal or the Azure CLI to define alert criteria, including metric thresholds, query results, and log analytics. By specifying conditions such as CPU usage exceeding a certain percentage or response time exceeding a specified threshold, organizations can ensure timely detection of performance degradation or system failures. Alerts can be configured to trigger notifications via various channels, including email, SMS, and webhook integrations, ensuring that relevant stakeholders are promptly informed of any issues. Additionally, organizations can configure alerts to trigger automated responses or remediation actions, such as scaling out resources or restarting failed services. By automating response actions, organizations can minimize downtime and mitigate the impact of performance issues on users and business operations. When configuring alerts for resilience monitoring, organizations should consider defining alerts for key performance indicators (KPIs) related to system reliability and availability. For example, organizations may want to set up alerts for metrics such as application availability, database latency, or network throughput. By monitoring these KPIs, organizations can identify potential issues that may affect system availability and take proactive measures to address them. Azure Monitor allows organizations to define alert rules based on a wide range of metrics and telemetry data collected from Azure resources and applications. Organizations can also leverage Azure Application Insights to monitor the performance and availability of web applications and define custom alerts for specific application metrics, such as page load time or server response time. By configuring alerts for resilience monitoring, organizations can detect and respond to issues affecting system* availability before they impact users and business operations. In addition to resilience monitoring, organizations should also configure alerts for performance monitoring to ensure optimal system performance and responsiveness. Performance alerts can be configured to notify organizations of potential performance degradation or bottlenecks that may affect user experience or application responsiveness. For example, organizations may want to set up alerts for metrics such as CPU usage, memory utilization, or disk I/O latency. By monitoring these performance metrics, organizations can identify performance bottlenecks and take corrective actions to optimize system performance and responsiveness. Azure Monitor provides built-in support for monitoring a wide range of performance metrics across Azure resources and applications. Organizations can use Azure Monitor to define custom alert rules for performance metrics and configure notifications to alert relevant stakeholders of performance issues. By configuring alerts for performance monitoring, organizations can proactively identify and address performance issues to ensure optimal system performance and user experience. In summary, configuring alerts for resilience and performance monitoring is essential for maintaining the reliability, availability, and performance of software applications and infrastructure. Azure Monitor *provides a powerful alerting mechanism that allows organizations to define custom alert rules based on specific conditions and thresholds. By configuring alerts for resilience monitoring, organizations can detect and respond to issues affecting system availability before they impact users and business operations. Similarly, by configuring alerts for performance monitoring, organizations can proactively identify and address performance issues to ensure optimal system performance and user experience. With the right alerting strategy in place, organizations can minimize downtime, optimize performance, and deliver a superior user experience.*

Chapter 10: Case Studies: Real-World Scalability and Resilience Implementations

Case studies of scalability and resilience challenges provide valuable insights into real-world scenarios where organizations have faced and overcome significant obstacles in managing their software systems. One such case study involves a large e-commerce company that experienced a surge in traffic during a major sales event, resulting in system outages and degraded performance. The company's infrastructure was not designed to handle such a high volume of concurrent users, leading to scalability issues and service disruptions.

To address the challenge, the company implemented auto-scaling capabilities in its cloud infrastructure, allowing it to dynamically provision additional resources to handle peak loads automatically. By leveraging auto-scaling, the company was able to maintain system availability and performance during peak traffic periods, ensuring a seamless shopping experience for customers. Another case study involves a software-as-a-service (SaaS) provider that experienced frequent downtime and service disruptions due to infrastructure failures and resource constraints. The provider's infrastructure was not resilient to failures, leading to prolonged outages and customer dissatisfaction. To improve resilience, the provider implemented a multi-region architecture with active-active failover capabilities, allowing it to distribute traffic across multiple data centers and regions. By deploying redundant infrastructure in geographically dispersed locations, the provider was able to mitigate the impact of infrastructure failures and ensure high availability for its services. Additionally, the provider implemented automated disaster recovery procedures to replicate data and configurations across multiple regions, enabling rapid failover in the event of a catastrophic failure.

These case studies highlight the importance of designing scalable and resilient architectures to meet the demands of modern software systems. By implementing auto-scaling, multi-region architectures, and automated disaster recovery procedures, organizations can ensure high availability and performance for their services, even in the face of unexpected challenges and failures. In another case study, a social media platform experienced performance degradation and downtime during peak usage periods, such as major sporting events or holidays. The platform's monolithic architecture was unable to scale efficiently to handle the increased load, resulting in slow response times and service interruptions. To address the issue, the platform migrated to a microservices architecture, breaking down its monolithic application into smaller, independently deployable services. By decoupling components and scaling each service independently, the platform was able to distribute load more effectively and improve overall system performance. Additionally, the platform implemented caching mechanisms and content delivery networks (CDNs) to reduce latency and improve the user experience for customers accessing media-rich content. The migration to a microservices architecture enabled the platform to scale more efficiently and handle peak traffic loads without sacrificing performance or reliability.

In summary, case studies of scalability and resilience challenges illustrate the importance of adopting modern architectural principles and best practices to address the complexities of today's software systems. By designing scalable and resilient architectures, leveraging cloud-native technologies, and implementing automated scaling and failover mechanisms, organizations can overcome scalability and resilience challenges and deliver a seamless user experience for their customers. Lessons learned and best practices from real-world implementations offer valuable insights into the challenges and successes encountered by *organizations in deploying and managing software systems. One key lesson learned is the importance of thorough planning and preparation before embarking on a DevOps transformation journey. Organizations that invest time and resources in defining clear objectives, establishing measurable goals, and aligning stakeholders' expectations are better equipped to navigate the complexities of DevOps adoption and implementation. Another crucial lesson is the significance of cultural transformation and organizational change management in driving successful DevOps initiatives. Organizations that foster a culture of collaboration, experimentation, and continuous improvement are more likely to succeed in implementing DevOps practices and achieving business agility. To facilitate cultural transformation, organizations can leverage techniques such as executive sponsorship, employee training, and cross-functional team collaboration to foster a culture of trust, transparency, and innovation. Additionally, organizations must prioritize communication and collaboration across teams and departments to break down silos and facilitate knowledge sharing and collaboration. By fostering a culture of open communication and collaboration, organizations can accelerate the adoption of DevOps practices and drive continuous improvement and innovation. One best practice derived from real-world implementations is the adoption of automation to streamline and standardize development, testing, deployment, and operations processes. Organizations that embrace automation tools and techniques such as infrastructure as code (IaC), continuous integration (CI), and continuous deployment (CD) can achieve greater efficiency, consistency, and reliability in their software delivery pipelines. To implement automation effectively, organizations can use tools such as Ansible, Terraform, and Puppet to automate the provisioning and configuration of infrastructure and environments. By automating repetitive tasks and manual processes, organizations can free up resources to focus on higher-value activities, such as innovation and product development. Furthermore, organizations can leverage automation to enforce best practices, compliance policies, and security controls across their software development lifecycle. By integrating automated testing, code analysis, and security scanning into their CI/CD pipelines, organizations can detect and address issues early in the development process, reducing the risk of security vulnerabilities and defects reaching production environments. Another best practice from real-world implementations is the adoption of cloud-native technologies and services to build scalable, resilient, and cost-effective solutions. Organizations that embrace cloud computing* platforms such as Microsoft Azure, Amazon Web Services (AWS), and Google Cloud Platform (GCP) can leverage a wide range of managed services and capabilities to accelerate their DevOps initiatives. To deploy cloud-native solutions effectively, organizations can use CLI commands to provision and configure resources such as virtual machines, containers, databases, and storage services. By leveraging cloud-native technologies such as Kubernetes, Docker, and serverless computing, organizations can build scalable and resilient applications that can handle unpredictable workloads and maintain high availability and performance. Additionally, organizations can take advantage of cloud-native monitoring, logging, and analytics services to gain real-time visibility into the health and performance of their applications and infrastructure. By leveraging cloud-native technologies and services, organizations can achieve greater agility, scalability, and innovation, enabling them to respond quickly to changing market demands and deliver value to their customers faster. In summary, lessons learned and best practices from real-world implementations provide valuable guidance and insights for organizations embarking on their DevOps journey. By prioritizing cultural transformation, embracing automation, and leveraging cloud-native technologies, organizations can overcome challenges and achieve success in *their DevOps initiatives. With a focus on continuous improvement and innovation, organizations can build resilient, scalable, and high-performing software systems that drive business growth and competitiveness in today's digital economy.*

BOOK 4
DEVOPS EXPERT
ACHIEVING MASTERY IN AZURE DEVOPS AND BEYOND - EXAM AZ-400

ROB BOTWRIGHT

Chapter 1: Beyond the Basics: Advanced Azure DevOps Concepts

Exploring advanced Azure DevOps features opens up a world of possibilities for organizations seeking to optimize their software development and delivery processes. One such feature is Azure Boards, a powerful agile project management tool that allows teams to plan, track, and collaborate on work items and tasks throughout the software development lifecycle. Using Azure Boards, teams can create and prioritize user stories, bugs, and tasks, assign work to team members, and track progress using customizable dashboards and reports. To leverage Azure Boards effectively, teams can use CLI commands to create and manage work items, query work item data, and automate common tasks such as assigning work items or updating status. By integrating Azure Boards with other Azure DevOps services such as Repos, Pipelines, and Test Plans, teams can establish end-to-end traceability and visibility into the entire software delivery process. Another advanced feature of Azure DevOps is Azure Repos, a Git-based version control system that allows teams to collaborate on code and manage software repositories securely. Azure Repos provides features such as branching, merging, and code reviews, enabling teams to maintain code quality and consistency throughout the development lifecycle. To deploy Azure Repos, teams can use CLI commands to create and clone repositories, push and pull changes, and manage branches and commits. By leveraging Azure Repos, teams can implement branching strategies such as GitFlow or GitHub Flow to manage feature development, hotfixes, and release cycles effectively. Additionally, teams can use Azure Repos to integrate with popular Git clients and IDEs, enabling seamless collaboration and code sharing across distributed teams. Azure Pipelines is another advanced feature of Azure DevOps that empowers teams to automate their build, test, and deployment processes. Azure Pipelines provides a flexible and customizable CI/CD platform that supports a wide range of programming languages, frameworks, and platforms. Using Azure Pipelines, teams can define pipelines as code using YAML syntax, enabling version-controlled, repeatable, and reproducible builds and deployments. To deploy Azure Pipelines, teams can use CLI commands to define pipeline configurations, trigger builds and releases, and monitor pipeline execution and results. By integrating Azure Pipelines with Azure Repos, teams can automate the entire software delivery process from code commit to production deployment, ensuring consistency, reliability, and traceability across environments. Azure Test Plans is another advanced feature of Azure DevOps that enables teams to plan, execute, and track manual and exploratory testing efforts. Azure Test Plans provides a centralized platform for managing test cases, test suites, and test plans, enabling teams to collaborate on testing activities and track test coverage and results. To deploy Azure Test Plans, teams can use CLI commands to create test plans, define test cases, and assign test tasks to team members. By integrating Azure Test Plans with Azure Boards and Azure Repos, teams can establish end-to-end traceability and visibility into testing efforts, ensuring comprehensive test coverage and timely detection of defects. Azure Artifacts is another advanced feature of Azure DevOps that enables teams to manage and share package dependencies and artifacts securely. Azure Artifacts provides a private, hosted package feed that allows teams to publish, store, and consume packages such as NuGet, npm, Maven, and Docker. To deploy Azure Artifacts, teams can use CLI commands to publish and manage packages, configure access permissions, and integrate with build and release pipelines. By leveraging Azure Artifacts, teams can streamline package management, reduce dependency management overhead, and improve build and deployment efficiency. In summary, exploring advanced Azure DevOps features empowers teams to optimize their software development and delivery processes, streamline collaboration, and improve productivity and quality. By leveraging Azure Boards, Azure Repos, Azure Pipelines, Azure Test Plans, and Azure Artifacts, teams can establish end-to-end traceability and visibility into their software delivery lifecycle, enabling them to deliver high-quality software faster and more reliably. With a focus on automation, collaboration, and continuous improvement, organizations can unlock the full potential of Azure DevOps and accelerate their digital transformation journey. Applying advanced techniques in Azure DevOps workflows is essential for organizations aiming to maximize efficiency and streamline their software development processes. One such technique is the use of multi-stage pipelines, which allow teams to define complex workflows consisting of multiple stages, each performing specific tasks such as building, testing, and deploying applications. To implement multi-stage pipelines, teams can use CLI commands to define pipeline configurations in YAML format, specifying stages, jobs, and tasks to be executed sequentially or in parallel. By leveraging multi-stage pipelines, teams can automate and orchestrate the entire software delivery process, from code commit to production deployment, with greater flexibility and control. Another advanced technique is the use of deployment strategies such as rolling deployments, canary deployments, and blue-green deployments to minimize downtime and mitigate risk during the deployment process. To implement deployment strategies in Azure DevOps, teams can use CLI commands to define deployment configurations, specify deployment targets, and control traffic routing between different deployment environments. By leveraging deployment strategies, teams can achieve zero-downtime deployments, reduce the impact of potential issues on end users, and ensure seamless delivery of new features and updates. Continuous integration (CI) and continuous deployment (CD) are fundamental principles of modern software development, and Azure DevOps provides robust support for automating CI/CD pipelines. To implement CI/CD pipelines in Azure DevOps, teams can use CLI commands to define pipeline configurations, trigger builds and releases based on code changes, and monitor pipeline execution and results. By embracing CI/CD practices, teams can accelerate the delivery of high-quality software, reduce manual intervention, and improve overall productivity and efficiency. Another advanced technique is the use of infrastructure as code (IaC) to automate the provisioning and configuration of infrastructure resources using declarative templates. In Azure DevOps, teams can use tools such as Azure Resource Manager (ARM) templates, Terraform, or Ansible to define infrastructure configurations as code and manage infrastructure deployments alongside application code. By adopting IaC, teams can achieve greater consistency, repeatability, and scalability in their infrastructure deployments, reduce the risk of configuration drift, and improve the overall reliability and resilience of their applications. Containerization is another advanced technique that enables teams to package applications and their dependencies into lightweight, portable containers that can run consistently across different environments. In Azure DevOps, teams can use Docker and Kubernetes to build, deploy, and manage containerized applications with ease. To deploy containerized applications in Azure DevOps, teams can use CLI commands to define Dockerfiles, build Docker images, and deploy containers to Kubernetes clusters or Azure Container Instances. By leveraging containerization, teams can achieve greater agility, scalability, and resource utilization, enabling them to deliver applications faster and more efficiently. Another advanced technique is the use of infrastructure monitoring and observability to gain insights into the health, performance, and availability of applications and infrastructure resources. In Azure DevOps, teams can use tools such as Azure Monitor, Application Insights, and Log Analytics to collect, analyze, and visualize telemetry *data from applications and infrastructure components. By leveraging monitoring and observability, teams can detect and troubleshoot issues proactively, optimize performance and resource utilization, and ensure a seamless end-user experience. In summary, applying advanced techniques in Azure DevOps workflows empowers teams to optimize their software development processes, automate repetitive tasks, and deliver high-quality software with speed and confidence. By embracing multi-stage pipelines, deployment strategies, CI/CD practices, infrastructure as code, containerization, and monitoring and observability, teams can achieve greater agility, scalability, and reliability in their software delivery lifecycle. With a focus on continuous improvement and innovation, organizations can unlock the full potential of Azure DevOps and accelerate their digital transformation journey.*

Chapter 2: DevOps Culture and Organizational Transformation

Understanding DevOps culture is essential for organizations striving to transform their software development and delivery practices and achieve greater agility, collaboration, and innovation. DevOps is not merely a set of tools or practices; it is a cultural mindset that emphasizes collaboration, communication, and shared responsibility between development and operations teams. To foster a DevOps culture, organizations must embrace principles such as empathy, transparency, and continuous improvement, creating an environment where teams can work together seamlessly towards common goals. CLI commands are instrumental in facilitating collaboration and communication within DevOps teams, enabling them to automate repetitive tasks, share knowledge, and streamline workflows. By leveraging CLI commands to automate infrastructure provisioning, configuration management, and deployment processes, teams can reduce manual intervention, minimize errors, and accelerate time-to-market. DevOps culture emphasizes the importance of breaking down silos and fostering cross-functional collaboration and accountability across development, operations, and other business units. By breaking down traditional barriers between teams and promoting collaboration and transparency, organizations can accelerate the delivery of high-quality software and respond more effectively to changing customer needs and market demands. CLI commands play a crucial role in promoting collaboration within DevOps teams, enabling developers, operations engineers, and other stakeholders to collaborate seamlessly on code, infrastructure, and deployment processes. By using CLI commands to automate tasks such as code reviews, testing, and deployment, teams can improve collaboration, increase productivity, and deliver value to customers more quickly. DevOps culture encourages a shift-left approach to software development, where testing, security, and other quality assurance activities are integrated early into the development lifecycle. By embracing practices such as continuous integration, continuous delivery, and continuous testing, organizations can identify and address issues earlier in the development process, reducing the risk of defects and improving software quality.

CLI commands are instrumental in enabling organizations to implement a shift-left approach to software development, allowing teams to automate testing, security scans, and other quality assurance activities as part of their CI/CD pipelines. By using

CLI commands to automate the execution of tests, scans, and other quality assurance activities, teams can accelerate feedback loops, identify and address issues earlier, and deliver higher-quality software more consistently. DevOps culture emphasizes the importance of feedback and continuous learning, where teams regularly reflect on their processes, gather insights from metrics and telemetry data, and experiment with new ideas and approaches to improve their practices. By fostering a culture of continuous learning and experimentation, organizations can adapt to change more effectively, innovate faster, and stay ahead of the competition. CLI commands play a crucial role in enabling organizations to gather insights from metrics and telemetry data, allowing teams to monitor the performance, availability, and reliability of their applications and infrastructure in real-time. By using CLI commands to collect and analyze metrics, teams can identify trends, patterns, and anomalies, gain insights into the health and performance of their systems, and make data-driven decisions to optimize their practices. DevOps culture emphasizes the importance of automation, where repetitive tasks, manual interventions, and bottlenecks are identified and automated to improve efficiency, consistency, and reliability. By automating tasks such as infrastructure provisioning, configuration management, and deployment processes, organizations can reduce human error, minimize downtime, and accelerate time-to-market. CLI commands are essential in enabling organizations to automate their DevOps processes, allowing teams to script and orchestrate tasks, workflows, and deployments across hybrid and multi-cloud environments. By using CLI commands to automate tasks such as infrastructure provisioning, configuration management, and application deployment, teams can achieve greater consistency, repeatability, and scalability in their operations. In summary, understanding DevOps culture is essential for organizations seeking to transform their software development and delivery practices and achieve greater agility, collaboration, and innovation.

By embracing principles such as collaboration, transparency, and continuous improvement, organizations can foster a culture of shared responsibility and accountability, enabling them to deliver value to customers more quickly and reliably.CLI commands play a crucial role in enabling organizations to automate their DevOps processes, allowing teams to streamline workflows, reduce manual intervention, and accelerate time-to-market. By leveraging CLI commands to automate tasks such as infrastructure provisioning, configuration management, and deployment processes, teams can achieve greater efficiency, consistency, and reliability in their operations. Strategies for organizational transformation towards DevOps involve a holistic approach that encompasses cultural, process, and technological changes to enable organizations to embrace DevOps principles effectively. CLI commands play a crucial role in facilitating organizational transformation by enabling automation, collaboration, and agility in software development and delivery processes. One strategy for organizational transformation towards DevOps is to foster a culture of collaboration and shared responsibility across development, operations, and other business units. This involves breaking down silos, promoting cross-functional teams, and encouraging open communication and transparency. CLI commands can support this strategy by allowing teams to automate tasks, share knowledge, and streamline workflows, enabling them to work together more effectively towards common goals. Another strategy is to implement Agile practices such as iterative development, frequent feedback, and continuous improvement, which align closely with DevOps principles. By adopting Agile practices, organizations can increase flexibility, responsiveness, and adaptability, enabling them to deliver value to customers more quickly and reliably. CLI commands can help organizations implement Agile practices by automating tasks such as backlog management, sprint planning, and release management, allowing teams to focus on delivering value to customers. Additionally, organizations can leverage CLI commands to integrate Agile tools such as Jira, Trello, or Azure Boards into their DevOps workflows, enabling seamless collaboration and visibility across teams. Implementing DevOps practices such as continuous integration, continuous delivery, and infrastructure as code (IaC) is another key strategy for organizational transformation. Continuous integration involves automating the process of integrating code changes into a shared repository and running automated tests to ensure code quality and reliability.

CLI commands can support continuous integration by allowing teams to automate tasks such as code compilation, unit testing, and code analysis, enabling them to detect and address issues early in the development process. Continuous delivery involves automating the process of deploying code changes to production or staging environments in a reliable and repeatable manner. CLI commands can help organizations implement continuous delivery by automating tasks such as building artifacts, provisioning infrastructure, and deploying applications, enabling them to release software more frequently and reliably. Infrastructure as code

(IaC) involves managing infrastructure resources using code-based definitions, enabling organizations to automate the provisioning, configuration, and management of infrastructure resources. CLI commands are essential for implementing infrastructure as code, allowing teams to define infrastructure configurations in code, version control infrastructure changes, and provision infrastructure resources using automation tools such as Terraform, Ansible, or Azure CLI. Another strategy for organizational transformation towards DevOps is to establish a culture of experimentation and continuous learning, where teams are encouraged to try new ideas, experiment with new technologies, and learn from failures.

CLI commands can support this strategy by enabling teams to automate tasks, iterate quickly, and gather feedback from users, enabling them to innovate faster and deliver value to customers more effectively. Additionally, organizations can leverage CLI commands to integrate monitoring and observability tools such as Prometheus, Grafana, or Azure Monitor into their DevOps workflows, enabling teams to gather insights into the health, performance, and reliability of their applications and infrastructure in real-time. In summary, strategies for organizational transformation towards DevOps involve a combination of cultural, process, and technological changes aimed at fostering collaboration, agility, and innovation. CLI commands play a crucial role in enabling organizations to automate tasks, streamline workflows, and accelerate time-to-market, enabling them to embrace DevOps principles effectively and deliver value to customers more quickly and reliably.

Chapter 3: Implementing Infrastructure as Code (IaC) with Azure DevOps

Introduction to Infrastructure as Code (IaC) is pivotal in modern software development and operations, revolutionizing the way organizations manage and provision infrastructure resources. CLI commands play a crucial role in implementing IaC, enabling developers and operators to define infrastructure configurations as code and automate their deployment and management. By treating infrastructure as code, organizations can achieve greater consistency, reliability, and scalability in their operations. The concept of Infrastructure as Code involves managing infrastructure resources such as virtual machines, networks, and storage using code-based definitions, rather than manual processes or graphical user interfaces. CLI commands are instrumental in implementing Infrastructure as Code, allowing organizations to define infrastructure configurations in a human-readable format, such as YAML or JSON, and automate the provisioning and management of infrastructure resources using tools such as Terraform, Ansible, or Azure CLI. The shift towards Infrastructure as Code has been driven by the need for greater agility, flexibility, and efficiency in managing modern, cloud-native applications and infrastructure. CLI commands provide a powerful interface for interacting with cloud providers' APIs and services, enabling organizations to automate tasks such as provisioning virtual machines, configuring networks, and deploying applications with ease. One of the key benefits of Infrastructure as Code is the ability to define infrastructure configurations in a version-controlled repository, allowing teams to track changes, collaborate more effectively, and maintain a reliable and auditable record of infrastructure changes over time. CLI commands facilitate version control workflows by allowing developers and operators to interact with version control systems such as Git, enabling them to commit, push, pull, and merge changes to infrastructure configurations with ease. Another benefit of Infrastructure as Code is the ability to treat infrastructure configurations as code, applying software engineering best practices such as modularization, abstraction, and reusability to infrastructure codebases. CLI commands enable organizations to write infrastructure code using programming languages such as HCL (HashiCorp Configuration Language), YAML, or JSON, allowing them to leverage the power of software engineering principles to manage and maintain their infrastructure more effectively. Infrastructure as Code enables organizations to adopt a "self-service" model for provisioning and managing infrastructure resources, empowering development and operations teams to automate repetitive tasks, reduce manual intervention, and accelerate time-to-market. CLI commands play a crucial role in enabling self-service infrastructure provisioning and management, allowing teams to automate tasks such as provisioning virtual machines, configuring networks, and deploying applications using code-based definitions. By leveraging Infrastructure as Code and CLI commands, organizations can achieve greater agility, flexibility, and efficiency in managing their infrastructure, enabling them to respond more effectively to changing business requirements and market dynamics. One of the key principles of Infrastructure as Code is the concept of "immutable infrastructure," where infrastructure resources are treated as disposable and are replaced rather than modified when changes are required. CLI commands enable organizations to implement immutable infrastructure patterns by automating the provisioning and deployment of infrastructure resources in a consistent, repeatable, and reliable manner. Another principle of Infrastructure as Code is the idea of "declarative configuration," where infrastructure configurations are defined in a declarative manner, specifying the desired state of the infrastructure rather than the steps needed to achieve it. CLI commands support declarative *configuration patterns by allowing organizations to define infrastructure configurations using high-level abstractions and automation tools, enabling them to express their infrastructure requirements more concisely and intuitively. In summary, Introduction to Infrastructure as Code (IaC) is a transformative concept in modern software development and operations, enabling organizations to manage and provision infrastructure resources more efficiently and effectively. CLI commands play a crucial role in implementing Infrastructure as Code, enabling organizations to define infrastructure configurations as code and automate their deployment and management with ease. By embracing Infrastructure as Code and CLI commands, organizations can achieve greater agility, flexibility, and reliability in managing their infrastructure, empowering them to innovate and deliver value to customers more quickly and reliably. Implementing Infrastructure as Code (IaC) with Azure DevOps Pipelines is a fundamental practice for modernizing software development and operations workflows. CLI commands play a pivotal role in this process, enabling developers and operators to automate the deployment and management of infrastructure resources directly from their pipelines. The integration of IaC with Azure DevOps Pipelines streamlines the provisioning of infrastructure resources, enhances consistency,* and promotes collaboration across development and operations teams. Azure DevOps Pipelines support the execution of CLI commands as part of the pipeline steps, allowing for seamless integration of IaC tasks into the overall deployment process. Leveraging CLI commands within Azure DevOps Pipelines, developers and operators can define infrastructure configurations using tools such as Terraform or Azure Resource Manager (ARM) templates and automate the deployment of these configurations alongside application code. For example, to deploy infrastructure resources using Terraform in an Azure DevOps Pipeline, developers can use the Terraform CLI to initialize the Terraform configuration, plan the changes, and apply the configuration directly from the pipeline YAML file. This ensures that infrastructure changes are deployed in a consistent and repeatable manner as part of the continuous integration and continuous deployment (CI/CD) process. Additionally, CLI commands can be used to authenticate with Azure services and manage resource access and permissions within Azure DevOps Pipelines securely. By leveraging service principals or managed identities, developers can execute CLI commands within pipelines without exposing sensitive credentials, ensuring the security of their infrastructure deployment process. Furthermore, Azure DevOps Pipelines offer built-in support for managing pipeline secrets and securely passing them as environment variables to CLI commands, further enhancing the security posture of the deployment process. Implementing IaC with Azure DevOps Pipelines enables organizations to achieve greater agility and efficiency in managing their infrastructure resources. By codifying infrastructure configurations and automating their deployment using CLI commands within pipelines, organizations can accelerate the delivery of applications and infrastructure changes while reducing manual errors and inconsistencies. Moreover, the declarative nature of IaC allows teams to version control infrastructure configurations alongside application code, enabling them to track changes, roll back to previous states, and collaborate more effectively. In addition to Terraform, Azure DevOps Pipelines also support other IaC tools such as ARM templates, enabling organizations to choose the best fit for their requirements. CLI commands provide the flexibility to interact with different IaC tools and services within Azure DevOps Pipelines, allowing organizations to tailor their deployment workflows to their specific needs. For example, developers can use Azure CLI commands to create and manage Azure resources directly from pipelines, leveraging Azure Resource Manager templates or other declarative approaches for infrastructure provisioning. This flexibility empowers organizations *to adopt a multi-cloud strategy or integrate with existing on-premises infrastructure seamlessly. Implementing IaC with Azure DevOps Pipelines also fosters collaboration and alignment between development and operations teams. By codifying infrastructure configurations and automating their deployment alongside application code, organizations can break down silos and establish a culture of shared responsibility and collaboration across teams. CLI commands play a crucial role in enabling this collaboration by providing a unified interface for managing infrastructure resources within the pipeline environment. Furthermore, by leveraging infrastructure as code practices within Azure DevOps Pipelines, organizations can establish consistent deployment patterns and best practices across projects and teams, driving operational excellence and reducing the risk of misconfigurations and errors. In summary, implementing Infrastructure as Code (IaC) with Azure DevOps Pipelines offers numerous benefits for organizations seeking to modernize their software development and operations workflows. CLI commands serve as a powerful tool for automating infrastructure deployment tasks within pipelines, enabling organizations to achieve greater agility, consistency, and collaboration in managing their infrastructure resources. By integrating IaC practices with Azure DevOps Pipelines, organizations can accelerate the delivery of applications and infrastructure changes, reduce manual errors, and foster a culture of collaboration and shared responsibility across development and operations teams.*

Chapter 4: Advanced Release Management Strategies

Advanced release management techniques play a pivotal role in modern software development practices, facilitating the seamless and efficient delivery of software products to end-users. In the context of Azure DevOps, release management encompasses a range of strategies and tools aimed at orchestrating the deployment of applications across different environments while ensuring reliability, consistency, and compliance. CLI commands are often utilized to automate various aspects of the release management process within Azure DevOps pipelines, enabling teams to streamline their deployment workflows and accelerate time-to-market for new features and updates. One advanced release management technique is environment-based release orchestration, where deployments are tailored to specific environments based on their unique requirements and characteristics. This approach involves defining separate release pipelines for each environment, such as development, staging, and production, and configuring the deployment process to account for differences in infrastructure, configuration, and testing procedures. CLI commands can be used to define and manage these environment-specific release pipelines within Azure DevOps, allowing teams to customize deployment workflows and ensure consistency across environments. Another key aspect of advanced release management is the implementation of release gates and approval workflows, which provide mechanisms for validating deployments before they are promoted to subsequent environments. Release gates can include automated tests, manual approvals, or external checks that must pass before a deployment can proceed, helping to mitigate risks and ensure the stability of production environments. CLI commands can be integrated into release pipelines to trigger these gates and facilitate the execution of validation tasks, such as running automated test suites or obtaining approvals from stakeholders. Additionally, advanced release management techniques often involve the use of deployment strategies to control the rollout of changes and minimize disruption to end-users. Common deployment strategies include rolling deployments, blue-green deployments, and canary releases, each offering different trade-offs in terms of risk mitigation, downtime, and performance impact. CLI commands can be leveraged to implement these deployment strategies within Azure DevOps pipelines, allowing teams to automate the process of provisioning and configuring infrastructure, deploying application artifacts, and monitoring the health of deployments in real-time. Furthermore, advanced release management techniques encompass the use of release templates and versioning schemes to manage the lifecycle of release artifacts and ensure traceability and reproducibility across environments. Release templates define the structure and configuration of release pipelines, including stages, tasks, and variables, while versioning schemes enable teams to track changes to release artifacts and dependencies over time. CLI commands enable teams to define and manage release templates and versioning schemes within Azure DevOps, providing a flexible and scalable approach to release management. Another important aspect of advanced release management is the integration of release analytics and insights, which provide visibility into the performance and success of deployments and help teams identify areas for improvement. Release analytics tools can track key metrics such as deployment frequency, lead time, and change failure rate, allowing teams to measure the effectiveness of their release processes and make data-driven decisions to optimize performance. CLI commands can be used to extract and analyze release data from Azure DevOps, enabling teams to generate reports, visualize trends, and identify patterns that impact release quality

and reliability. Additionally, advanced release management encompasses the implementation of compliance and governance controls to ensure that deployments adhere to organizational policies, regulatory requirements, and industry standards. This may include enforcing access controls, implementing security checks, and maintaining audit trails of release activities. CLI commands can be utilized to define and enforce compliance policies within Azure DevOps pipelines, enabling teams to automate the validation and enforcement of security and compliance requirements throughout the release process. In summary, advanced release management techniques play a critical role in enabling organizations to deliver high-quality software products efficiently and reliably. By leveraging CLI commands within Azure DevOps pipelines, teams can automate and streamline their release processes, implement sophisticated deployment strategies, and ensure compliance with organizational policies and industry standards. By embracing advanced release management practices, organizations can accelerate time-to-market, improve release quality, and enhance the overall agility and competitiveness of their software delivery pipelines.
Streamlining release processes is essential for modern software development teams seeking to deliver high-quality products efficiently and

consistently. Within the realm of software development, release management encompasses a series of activities aimed at planning, scheduling, and coordinating the deployment of software applications and updates to production environments. In the context of Azure DevOps, streamlining release processes involves leveraging its suite of tools and capabilities to automate and orchestrate the various stages of the release lifecycle. CLI commands are frequently utilized to interact with Azure DevOps services and resources, enabling teams to automate repetitive tasks and streamline release workflows. One fundamental aspect of streamlining release processes with Azure DevOps is the adoption of continuous integration (CI) practices. CI involves automating the integration of code changes into a shared repository, followed by the execution of automated tests and code quality checks to validate the changes. CLI commands can be used to configure CI pipelines within Azure DevOps, defining triggers that automatically initiate builds whenever new code is pushed to the repository. By automating the build and test process, teams can detect and address issues early in the development cycle, reducing the risk of defects and ensuring that code changes are always in a deployable state. Another key component of streamlining release processes is the implementation of continuous deployment (CD) practices. CD extends the principles of CI by automating the deployment of code changes to production environments, ensuring that updates are delivered to end-users quickly and reliably. In Azure DevOps, CD pipelines can be configured to deploy applications automatically based on predefined criteria, such as passing automated tests and obtaining approvals from stakeholders. CLI commands enable teams to define CD pipelines within Azure DevOps, specifying deployment targets, configuring release triggers, and orchestrating complex deployment workflows. By automating the deployment process, teams can minimize manual intervention, reduce the risk of human error, and accelerate the delivery of new features and updates to customers. Additionally, streamlining release processes with Azure DevOps involves the use of release gates and approval workflows to enforce quality control and ensure compliance with organizational policies. Release gates are conditions that must be satisfied before a deployment can proceed, such as passing automated tests, obtaining approvals from designated approvers, or meeting compliance requirements. CLI commands can be employed to define and manage release gates within Azure DevOps, enabling teams to enforce checks and balances throughout the release process. By incorporating release gates and approval workflows into release pipelines, teams can maintain visibility and control over the deployment process, mitigating risks and ensuring that only verified changes are promoted to production environments. Furthermore, streamlining release processes requires the adoption of infrastructure as code (IaC) principles to automate the provisioning and configuration of infrastructure resources. IaC involves defining infrastructure configurations in human-readable code files, which can be version-controlled, tested, and deployed alongside application code. CLI commands can be utilized to interact with infrastructure as code tools and platforms within Azure DevOps, such as Azure Resource Manager (ARM) templates or Terraform scripts, enabling teams to provision and manage infrastructure resources programmatically. By treating infrastructure as code, teams can achieve consistency, repeatability, and scalability in their release processes, reducing the time and effort required to deploy and manage infrastructure environments. Additionally, streamlining release processes with Azure DevOps involves the integration of monitoring and logging solutions to provide visibility into the health and performance of deployed applications. Monitoring tools such as Azure Monitor enable teams to collect and analyze telemetry data from applications and infrastructure, detecting issues and identifying performance *bottlenecks in real-time. CLI commands can be employed to configure monitoring alerts and dashboards within Azure DevOps, enabling teams to receive notifications and visualize key metrics related to application health and performance. By integrating monitoring and logging solutions into release pipelines, teams can proactively identify and resolve issues, ensuring that applications meet service level objectives (SLOs) and deliver a seamless user experience. Additionally, streamlining release processes with Azure DevOps involves the adoption of best practices for security and compliance to protect sensitive data and mitigate security risks. Security controls such as role-based access control (RBAC), encryption, and network security groups can be implemented to secure Azure DevOps resources and prevent unauthorized access. CLI commands can be used to configure security policies and settings within Azure DevOps, enabling teams to enforce security best practices and comply with regulatory requirements. By integrating security and compliance into release pipelines, teams can minimize the risk of security breaches and ensure the integrity and confidentiality of sensitive data. Moreover, streamlining release processes with Azure DevOps entails the implementation of automated testing practices to validate application functionality and performance. Automated tests, including unit tests, integration tests, and end-to-*

end tests, can be executed as part of CI/CD pipelines to verify that code changes meet quality standards and do not introduce regressions. CLI commands can be utilized to trigger automated tests within Azure DevOps, enabling teams to run tests in parallel, analyze test results, and identify failures quickly. By automating testing processes, teams can accelerate feedback loops, reduce manual effort, and improve the overall quality of releases. Additionally, streamlining release processes with Azure DevOps involves the use of release management templates and templates to standardize and templatize the configuration of release pipelines. Release management templates define the structure and configuration of release pipelines, including stages, tasks, and variables, while templates enable teams to reuse common configurations across multiple projects and environments. CLI commands can be employed to create and manage release management templates and templates within Azure DevOps, enabling teams to establish consistency and repeatability in their release processes. By leveraging templates and templates, teams can reduce manual effort, minimize errors, and ensure that releases adhere to organizational standards and best practices. In summary, streamlining release processes with Azure DevOps requires a holistic approach that encompasses automation, collaboration, and best practices across the entire release lifecycle. By leveraging CI/CD pipelines, release gates, infrastructure as code, monitoring and logging, security and compliance, automated testing, and release management templates and templates, teams can accelerate the delivery of high-quality software products while minimizing risks and ensuring compliance with regulatory requirements. CLI commands serve as a powerful tool for automating and orchestrating release processes within Azure DevOps, enabling teams to streamline workflows, improve efficiency, and deliver value to customers faster.

Chapter 5: Extending Azure DevOps with Custom Extensions and Integrations

Building custom extensions for Azure DevOps opens up a world of possibilities for extending the platform's capabilities and tailoring it to meet the specific needs of your organization. These extensions can range from simple integrations with external tools to complex solutions that add entirely new features to Azure DevOps. CLI commands are often used in the development and deployment of these custom extensions, enabling developers to interact with Azure DevOps services and resources programmatically. One of the first steps in building a custom extension is to define its requirements and scope, identifying the specific functionality it needs to deliver and the target audience it aims to serve. This initial planning phase is crucial for ensuring that the extension meets the needs of its intended users and aligns with broader organizational goals. Once the requirements are defined, the next step is to choose the appropriate technology stack for building the extension. Azure DevOps supports a variety of development frameworks and languages, including JavaScript, TypeScript, and .NET, allowing developers to leverage their existing skills and preferences. CLI commands can be used to set up the development environment, install necessary dependencies, and scaffold the initial project structure. With the development environment configured, developers can begin writing code to implement the desired functionality of the extension. This may involve interacting with Azure DevOps REST APIs to retrieve or manipulate data, creating user interface components using frameworks like React or Angular, or integrating with external services using webhooks or APIs. CLI commands can be used to manage the codebase, run automated tests, and package the extension for deployment. As the development progresses, it's essential to test the extension thoroughly to ensure its reliability, performance, and compatibility with different environments and configurations. Automated testing frameworks such as Jest or Mocha can be used to write and execute unit tests, integration tests, and end-to-end tests, verifying that the extension behaves as expected under various scenarios. CLI commands can be employed to trigger test runs, collect and analyze test results, and generate reports for review. In addition to functional testing, it's also important to consider the security implications of the custom extension. This includes implementing authentication and authorization mechanisms to control access to sensitive data and resources, as well as safeguarding against common security vulnerabilities such as cross-site scripting (XSS) or injection attacks. CLI commands can be utilized to configure security settings, enforce security policies, and perform security scans to identify potential vulnerabilities. Once the extension has been thoroughly tested and validated, it's time to package it for deployment to Azure DevOps. Extensions for Azure DevOps are typically packaged as Visual Studio Team Services (VSTS) extensions, which are distributed and installed from the Visual Studio Marketplace. CLI commands can be used to package the extension into a .vsix file, which contains all the necessary artifacts and metadata required for installation. The .vsix file can then be uploaded to the Visual Studio Marketplace, where it will undergo a review process before being published for public use. During the review process, the extension will be evaluated for compliance with Marketplace policies and guidelines, ensuring that it meets the quality and security standards expected by users. Once the extension is approved and published, it can be installed by users directly from the Visual Studio Marketplace or through the Azure DevOps portal. CLI commands can be used to manage the installation and configuration of the extension, including assigning permissions, enabling features, and configuring settings. After the extension is deployed, it's essential to monitor its usage and performance to identify any issues or *opportunities for improvement. CLI commands can be employed to collect telemetry data, monitor logs, and analyze usage patterns, providing valuable insights into how the extension is being used and where it can be optimized. Additionally, it's important to solicit feedback from users to gather input on their experience with the extension and identify areas for enhancement or refinement. CLI commands can be used to collect and analyze feedback, prioritize feature requests, and iterate on the extension based on user input. In summary, building custom extensions for Azure DevOps is a powerful way to extend the platform's capabilities and tailor it to meet the unique needs of your organization. By leveraging CLI commands and development best practices, developers can create extensions that add value, improve productivity, and enhance collaboration within their teams. Whether it's integrating with external tools, automating repetitive tasks, or adding new features, custom extensions have the potential to transform how teams work and deliver software.*

Integrating external tools and services with Azure DevOps can significantly enhance the capabilities and efficiency of your development workflow. CLI commands play a crucial role in facilitating this integration process by enabling developers to interact with Azure DevOps services and resources programmatically. One common scenario for integrating external tools with Azure DevOps is to streamline the build and release process by automating tasks such as code analysis, testing, and deployment. For example, you can use CLI commands to trigger a build pipeline in Azure DevOps whenever new code is pushed to a repository, or to automatically deploy a new version of an application to a staging environment after successful testing. By automating these tasks, you can reduce manual overhead and ensure consistent and reliable deployments across your development, testing, and production environments. Another use case for integrating external tools with Azure DevOps is to centralize project management and collaboration by connecting Azure DevOps with popular productivity tools such as Microsoft Teams, Slack, or Trello. CLI commands can be used to configure webhooks or API integrations that notify team members about important events in Azure DevOps, such as new work items being created, changes being made to the codebase, or builds and releases being completed. This helps to keep everyone on the team informed and aligned with the progress of the project, regardless of which tools they prefer to use. Additionally, integrating external testing and monitoring tools with Azure DevOps can help you gain deeper insights into the quality and performance of your applications. CLI commands can be used to set up continuous integration and continuous deployment (CI/CD) pipelines that automatically run tests and collect metrics at each stage of the development lifecycle. For example, you can use CLI commands to configure Azure DevOps to trigger automated functional tests whenever a new build is deployed to a testing environment, or to monitor the performance of your applications in production and alert you to any anomalies or issues. By integrating these tools and services with Azure DevOps, you can create a more holistic and data-driven approach to software development that enables you to identify and address issues earlier in the development process, resulting in higher-quality software and faster time to market. In addition to automating tasks and streamlining workflows, integrating external tools and services with Azure DevOps can also help you leverage the latest technologies and best practices in your development process. For example, you can use CLI commands to integrate Azure DevOps with cloud-based development environments such as Visual Studio Online or GitHub Codespaces, enabling your team to develop, test, and deploy applications entirely in the cloud. This can reduce the need for local development environments and make it easier for developers to collaborate and work from anywhere, on any device. Similarly, you can use CLI commands to integrate Azure DevOps with containerization and orchestration platforms such as Docker and Kubernetes, enabling you to build and deploy containerized applications more efficiently and consistently. By containerizing your applications, you can ensure that they run consistently across different environments and scale more easily to meet changing demand. This can be particularly useful for modern, microservices-based architectures where applications are composed of multiple independent services that need to be deployed and scaled independently. In summary, integrating external tools and services with Azure DevOps can help you streamline your development workflow, improve collaboration and communication, and leverage the latest technologies and best practices in your development process. CLI commands play a crucial role in enabling this integration by providing a powerful and flexible way to interact with Azure DevOps services and resources programmatically. Whether you're automating tasks, centralizing project management and collaboration, or leveraging the latest technologies and best practices, integrating external tools and services with Azure DevOps can help you build better software faster and more efficiently.

Chapter 6: Security and Compliance in DevOps Environments

Securing DevOps workflows is paramount in ensuring the integrity, confidentiality, and availability of your software development processes and assets. CLI commands are invaluable tools in implementing security measures within DevOps pipelines, allowing for the automation and enforcement of security best practices. One essential aspect of securing DevOps workflows is implementing robust access controls to limit who can view, modify, or execute pipelines and associated resources. CLI commands can be used to define role-based access controls (RBAC) in Azure DevOps, assigning specific permissions to individuals or groups based on their roles and responsibilities. For example, you can use the az devops security commands to manage permissions for users, groups, or service principals in Azure DevOps, ensuring that only authorized personnel have access to sensitive resources such as repositories, pipelines, and deployment environments. Another critical aspect of securing DevOps workflows is ensuring the integrity of your source code and pipeline configurations. CLI commands can be used to implement code signing and verification processes that validate the authenticity and integrity of code changes and pipeline configurations before they are deployed. For example, you can use the az pipelines runs tag add command to tag pipeline runs with a unique identifier generated using a cryptographic hash function such as SHA-256, providing a verifiable record of the code changes included in each run. Additionally, you can use the az pipelines runs list command to retrieve the tags associated with a pipeline run, enabling you to quickly identify and verify the integrity of code changes included in the deployment. Implementing secure coding practices is another essential aspect of securing DevOps workflows. CLI commands can be used to automate code analysis and vulnerability scanning processes that identify and remediate security vulnerabilities in your source code before they are deployed. For example, you can use the az pipelines build queue command to trigger a build pipeline in Azure DevOps that runs static code analysis tools such as SonarQube or ESLint, scanning your codebase for common security issues such as SQL injection, cross-site scripting (XSS), or insecure cryptographic algorithms. Additionally, you can use the az pipelines build logs command to retrieve the build logs generated by these tools, enabling you to review the results and take appropriate action to address any identified vulnerabilities before they are deployed. Securely managing secrets and sensitive configuration data is another critical aspect of securing DevOps workflows. CLI commands can be used to automate the retrieval and injection of secrets and configuration values into pipelines and deployment environments, reducing the risk of exposure and unauthorized access. For example, you can use the az pipelines variable-group variable list command to retrieve the values of variables defined in a variable group in Azure DevOps, enabling you to securely inject these values into your pipeline scripts at runtime. Additionally, you can use the az keyvault secret show command to retrieve secrets stored in Azure Key Vault, enabling you to securely retrieve sensitive configuration data such as database connection strings, API keys, or encryption keys and inject them into your pipeline scripts or deployment configurations. Implementing secure deployment practices is essential for ensuring the integrity and availability of your applications and services. CLI commands can be used to automate deployment processes and enforce security controls that mitigate the risk of unauthorized or malicious changes to your production environments. For example, you can use the az webapp deployment slot swap command to automate the deployment of application updates to Azure App Service deployment slots, enabling you to perform zero-downtime deployments by swapping the production and staging slots once the deployment is complete.

Additionally, you can use the az network nsg rule create command to create network security group (NSG) rules in Azure that restrict inbound and outbound traffic to your deployment environments, limiting the attack surface and reducing the risk of unauthorized access or data exfiltration. In summary, securing DevOps workflows requires a multi-faceted approach that addresses access control, code integrity, secure coding practices, secrets management, and secure deployment practices. CLI commands play a crucial role in implementing these security measures, enabling you to automate and enforce security best practices throughout the software development lifecycle. By leveraging CLI commands to implement robust security controls within your DevOps pipelines, you can reduce the risk of security breaches, data leaks, and service disruptions, ensuring the integrity, confidentiality, and availability of your applications and services.

Ensuring compliance in DevOps processes is crucial for organizations operating in regulated industries or those handling sensitive data. CLI commands are instrumental in implementing and enforcing compliance measures within DevOps workflows, facilitating automation and auditability. Compliance requirements vary depending on the industry and geographic location, necessitating a thorough understanding of relevant regulations and standards such as GDPR, HIPAA, PCI DSS, and SOC 2. CLI commands can be used to configure access controls, encryption, and monitoring mechanisms to align with compliance requirements. For example, organizations subject to GDPR can use the az storage account create command to enable encryption at rest for Azure Storage accounts, ensuring that data is protected according to GDPR's encryption requirements. Additionally, organizations subject to HIPAA can use the az webapp config set command to configure Azure App Service instances to use HTTPS with SSL/TLS encryption, ensuring the secure transmission of protected health information (PHI) over the internet. Implementing access controls is essential for ensuring compliance with regulatory requirements related to data privacy and confidentiality. CLI commands can be used to configure role-based access controls (RBAC) and resource locks to restrict access to sensitive resources and prevent unauthorized changes. For example, organizations subject to PCI DSS can use the az role assignment create command to assign specific roles such as "Reader" or "Contributor" to users or groups, limiting their access to PCI-related resources such as Azure SQL databases or storage accounts. Additionally, organizations subject to SOC 2 can use the az lock create command to apply resource locks to critical infrastructure components *such as virtual machines or network security groups, preventing unauthorized modifications or deletions that could impact compliance. Implementing audit trails and logging mechanisms is essential for demonstrating compliance with regulatory requirements related to data integrity and accountability. CLI commands can be used to configure diagnostic settings and logging options for Azure resources, enabling organizations to track and monitor changes to critical infrastructure components. For example, organizations subject to SOC 2 can use the az monitor diagnostic-settings create command to configure diagnostic settings for Azure resources such as virtual machines or Azure SQL databases, specifying which types of logs and metrics should be collected and stored for audit purposes. Additionally, organizations subject to GDPR can use the az monitor metrics alert create command to create alerts that notify administrators when suspicious or anomalous activities are detected, enabling them to investigate and respond to potential compliance violations proactively. Implementing data encryption is essential for ensuring compliance with regulatory requirements related to data protection and confidentiality. CLI commands can be used to configure encryption options for Azure resources such as virtual machines, storage accounts, and databases, ensuring that data is protected both at rest and in transit. For example, organizations subject to GDPR can use the az vm encryption enable command to enable encryption for virtual machines using Azure Disk Encryption, ensuring that sensitive data stored on disk is encrypted using industry-standard encryption algorithms such as AES-256. Additionally, organizations subject to HIPAA can use the az keyvault secret set command to store encryption keys securely in Azure Key Vault, ensuring that data encrypted with these keys remains protected according to HIPAA's encryption requirements. Implementing data retention policies is essential for ensuring compliance with regulatory requirements related to data retention and disposal. CLI commands can be used to configure data retention settings for Azure resources such as storage accounts and databases, specifying how long data should be retained before it is deleted or archived. For example, organizations subject to GDPR can use the az storage blob service-properties retention-policy command to configure a retention policy for Azure Blob Storage containers, specifying the retention period and whether data should be permanently deleted or archived after the retention period expires. Additionally, organizations subject to PCI DSS can use the az sql db audit-policy command to configure audit policies for Azure SQL databases, specifying which types of events should be audited and how long audit logs should be retained for* compliance purposes. Implementing change management processes is essential for ensuring compliance with regulatory requirements related to change control and documentation. CLI commands can be used to automate change management workflows and enforce approval processes for making changes to critical infrastructure components. For example, organizations subject to SOC 2 can use the az deployment group create command to deploy changes to Azure resources using Azure Resource Manager templates, enabling them to define and enforce approval gates for each stage of the deployment process. Additionally, organizations subject to ITIL or COBIT frameworks can use the az policy assignment create command to define policies that enforce change management controls for Azure resources, ensuring that changes are documented, reviewed, and approved before they are implemented in production environments. In summary, ensuring compliance in DevOps processes requires a comprehensive approach that encompasses access controls, audit trails, data encryption, data retention, and change management processes. CLI commands play a crucial role in implementing and enforcing compliance measures within DevOps workflows, enabling organizations to align with regulatory requirements and demonstrate adherence to industry standards and best practices. By leveraging

CLI commands to automate and enforce compliance measures, organizations can mitigate the risk of regulatory violations, data breaches, and financial penalties, ensuring the trust and confidence of customers, partners, and regulatory authorities.

Chapter 7: Advanced Monitoring and Analytics in Azure DevOps

Advanced monitoring tools are indispensable for maintaining the health, performance, and security of software systems deployed in Azure DevOps environments. Leveraging these tools requires a comprehensive understanding of their capabilities and how they can be integrated into DevOps workflows. CLI commands play a crucial role in configuring and managing these monitoring tools, enabling organizations to gain actionable insights into their applications and infrastructure. One of the key monitoring tools in Azure DevOps is Azure Monitor, which provides a unified platform for collecting, analyzing, and acting on telemetry data from applications and infrastructure. CLI commands can be used to configure Azure Monitor resources such as metrics, logs, alerts, and dashboards, allowing organizations to monitor the health and performance of their Azure resources in real-time. For example, organizations can use the az monitor metric alert create command to create alerts that notify administrators when predefined thresholds are exceeded for specific metrics, such as CPU utilization or memory usage on virtual machines. Additionally, organizations can use the az monitor log-analytics workspace create command to create a Log Analytics workspace, where they can centralize and analyze log data from multiple sources, including Azure resources, on-premises systems, and third-party applications. Another essential monitoring tool in Azure DevOps is Application Insights, which provides application performance monitoring (APM) and application analytics capabilities for web applications, APIs, and microservices. CLI commands can be used to configure Application Insights resources, instrument application code, and create custom dashboards and reports to monitor application performance and diagnose issues. For example, organizations can use the az resource create command to create an Application Insights resource and the az monitor app-insights component show command to retrieve the instrumentation key required to connect the application to the Application Insights service. Additionally, organizations can use the az monitor app-insights component feature set command to enable features such as distributed tracing, request tracking, and dependency tracking for their applications. Azure DevOps also integrates seamlessly with third-party monitoring tools such as Prometheus, Grafana, and Datadog, allowing organizations to leverage their existing investments in monitoring infrastructure. CLI commands can be used to deploy and configure these third-party monitoring tools in Azure DevOps environments, enabling organizations to monitor the health, performance, and security of their applications and infrastructure using familiar tools and workflows. For example, organizations can use the az acs kubernetes install-connector command to deploy the Prometheus connector for Azure Kubernetes Service (AKS) clusters, allowing them to collect and visualize metrics from Kubernetes pods and nodes using Prometheus and Grafana. Additionally, organizations can use the az datadog integration create command to create an integration between Azure DevOps and Datadog, allowing them to monitor Azure resources, track deployments, and analyze logs and metrics using the Datadog platform. In summary, leveraging advanced monitoring tools in Azure DevOps is essential for maintaining the health, performance, and security of software systems deployed in DevOps environments. CLI commands play a crucial role in configuring and managing these monitoring tools, enabling organizations to gain actionable insights into their applications and infrastructure and detect and resolve issues proactively. By integrating advanced monitoring tools into their DevOps workflows, organizations can improve the reliability, scalability, and efficiency of their software delivery pipelines and deliver better experiences for their customers.

Analyzing DevOps metrics is crucial for driving continuous improvement and optimizing software delivery processes. These metrics provide valuable insights into the performance, efficiency, and reliability of DevOps workflows, enabling organizations to identify bottlenecks, detect trends, and make data-driven decisions to enhance their software delivery pipelines. CLI commands play a significant role in collecting, aggregating, and visualizing DevOps metrics, allowing organizations to automate the monitoring and analysis process and gain actionable insights in real-time. One of the key metrics organizations track is cycle time, which measures the time it takes for a change to be implemented and deployed into production. CLI commands can be used to collect data on cycle time from various sources, including version control systems, build servers, and deployment pipelines. For example, organizations can use the git log command to retrieve commit history from a Git repository and calculate the time elapsed between code commits and deployments using timestamps. Additionally, organizations can use the az pipelines runs list command to list pipeline runs in Azure DevOps and retrieve information such as start and end times, duration, and success status to calculate cycle time metrics for their CI/CD pipelines. Another critical metric is deployment frequency, which measures how often changes are deployed into production. CLI commands can be used to track deployment frequency by counting the number of deployments performed within a specified time period. For example, organizations can use the az acs kubernetes get-credentials command to authenticate with an Azure Kubernetes Service (AKS) cluster and then use the Kubernetes API to query deployment objects and retrieve deployment history. Additionally, organizations can use the az monitor metrics list command to query Azure Monitor metrics for Azure resources such as virtual machines, containers, and databases and retrieve deployment-related metrics such as deployment count and success rate. Organizations also monitor metrics related to build and test automation to ensure the reliability and quality of their software releases. CLI commands can be used to collect data on build success rate, test coverage, and test pass rate from CI/CD pipelines and testing frameworks. For example, organizations can use the az pipelines build list command to list build runs in Azure DevOps and retrieve information such as build status, duration, and test results. Additionally, organizations can use the az test list command to list test runs in Azure DevOps and retrieve information such as test name, duration, and pass/fail status to calculate test-related metrics. CLI commands can also be used to aggregate and visualize DevOps metrics using tools such as

Grafana, Prometheus, and Power BI. For example, organizations can use the az monitor metrics list command to query Azure Monitor metrics and export the data to a CSV file, which can then be imported into Grafana or Power BI for analysis and visualization. Additionally, organizations can use the az monitor diagnostic-settings create command to configure diagnostic settings for Azure resources and send metric data to Azure Monitor, where it can be analyzed using built-in dashboards and queries. In summary, analyzing DevOps metrics is essential for driving continuous improvement and optimizing software delivery processes. CLI commands play a crucial role in collecting, aggregating, and visualizing DevOps metrics, allowing organizations to automate the monitoring and analysis process and gain actionable insights in real-time. By tracking metrics such as cycle time, deployment frequency, build success rate, and test coverage, organizations can identify areas for improvement, prioritize initiatives, and make data-driven decisions to enhance their software delivery pipelines and deliver better experiences for their customers.

Chapter 8: Implementing DevOps at Scale: Enterprise Considerations

Scaling DevOps practices for enterprise organizations presents unique challenges and opportunities compared to smaller teams or startups. CLI commands are indispensable tools in this endeavor, offering automation and efficiency in managing complex infrastructure and workflows. One of the key challenges in scaling DevOps for enterprise organizations is managing the complexity inherent in large-scale projects and teams. CLI commands provide a means to automate repetitive tasks, streamline processes, and enforce consistency across environments. For instance, using the Azure CLI, organizations can script the provisioning of resources, configuration of infrastructure, and deployment of applications, ensuring that deployments are consistent and reproducible across environments. Another challenge in scaling DevOps for enterprise organizations is ensuring collaboration and communication across distributed teams and departments. CLI commands can facilitate communication by providing a common interface for managing and monitoring DevOps workflows. For example, the Azure CLI allows teams to collaborate on infrastructure and application deployments by sharing scripts and automating routine tasks. Additionally, tools like Microsoft Teams can be integrated with CLI commands to enable real-time communication and collaboration among team members. Another challenge in scaling DevOps for enterprise organizations is managing security and compliance requirements. CLI commands can be used to enforce security policies, manage access controls, and audit system activity. For example, organizations can use the Azure CLI to configure network security groups, manage encryption keys, and monitor security alerts. Additionally, CLI commands can be integrated with compliance tools to automate the enforcement of regulatory requirements and ensure that deployments adhere to industry standards. Despite these challenges, scaling DevOps for enterprise organizations also presents significant opportunities for improving efficiency, reducing costs, and accelerating innovation. CLI commands enable organizations to automate manual processes, reduce human error, and increase productivity. For example, by scripting the deployment of infrastructure and applications, organizations can reduce deployment times from weeks to minutes, enabling faster time-to-market for new features and updates. Additionally, CLI commands can be integrated with monitoring and analytics tools to provide real-time insights into system performance, identify bottlenecks, and optimize resource utilization. In summary, scaling DevOps practices for enterprise organizations requires careful planning, collaboration, and automation. CLI commands play a crucial role in this process, providing a powerful toolset for managing complex infrastructure and workflows. By leveraging CLI commands to automate routine tasks, enforce security policies, and facilitate communication and collaboration, enterprise organizations can realize the full potential of DevOps and drive innovation at scale. Scaling DevOps brings its own set of challenges, especially as organizations expand and grow in size. CLI commands play a pivotal role in overcoming these challenges by providing automation and streamlining processes. One common challenge in scaling DevOps is maintaining consistency across diverse environments and teams. Using CLI commands, organizations can automate the provisioning and configuration of infrastructure, ensuring uniformity across different environments. For instance, with the AWS CLI, administrators can create and manage resources such as EC2 instances, S3 buckets, and RDS databases using scripts or commands, thus ensuring consistency across development, testing, and production environments. Another challenge in scaling DevOps is managing dependencies and version control across multiple projects and teams. CLI commands enable organizations to automate dependency management and version control processes, reducing manual errors and ensuring compatibility across different components. For example, with tools like Git and the Git CLI, teams can manage code repositories, track changes, and collaborate on code development seamlessly. Additionally, using version control systems like Git allows teams to roll back changes, merge branches, and track the history of code modifications, thereby facilitating collaboration and reducing the risk of conflicts. Scalability also brings challenges in terms of monitoring and troubleshooting complex systems. CLI commands empower organizations to automate monitoring tasks and gain real-time insights into system performance and health. For example, using monitoring tools like Prometheus and Grafana alongside CLI commands, organizations can set up automated alerts, create custom dashboards, and analyze metrics to identify and address performance issues proactively. Moreover, CLI commands can be used to automate incident response processes, enabling teams to troubleshoot and resolve issues more efficiently. Another significant challenge in scaling DevOps is ensuring security and compliance across distributed environments. CLI commands offer robust capabilities for implementing security controls, enforcing compliance policies, and managing access permissions. For instance, with tools like Terraform and the Terraform CLI, organizations can define infrastructure as code (IaC) templates to provision resources in a secure and compliant manner. By codifying security best practices into IaC templates, organizations can ensure that security controls are applied consistently across all environments, thereby mitigating risks and adhering to regulatory requirements. Collaboration and communication are essential for successful DevOps implementation, especially in large-scale environments. CLI commands facilitate collaboration by providing a common interface for teams to interact with infrastructure and applications. For example, using collaboration platforms like Slack and Microsoft Teams alongside CLI commands, teams can automate notifications, share status updates, and coordinate activities seamlessly. Additionally, CLI commands can be integrated with version control systems and issue tracking tools to streamline the development workflow further. One of the critical challenges in scaling DevOps is managing the cultural shift within the organization. CLI commands can be used to automate repetitive tasks, freeing up time for teams to focus on innovation and collaboration. Moreover, CLI commands enable organizations to implement DevOps practices incrementally, allowing teams to adopt new tools and processes at their own pace. By providing automation and standardization, CLI commands help organizations overcome resistance to change and foster a culture of continuous improvement. In summary, scaling DevOps presents several challenges, ranging from maintaining consistency across environments to ensuring security and compliance. CLI commands offer a powerful solution to these challenges by providing automation, standardization, and collaboration capabilities. By leveraging CLI commands effectively, organizations can overcome obstacles in scaling DevOps and accelerate their journey towards digital transformation.

Chapter 9: Continuous Learning and Improvement in DevOps Practices

Cultivating a culture of continuous learning is paramount in the ever-evolving landscape of DevOps. CLI commands serve as indispensable tools in fostering this culture, enabling teams to experiment, innovate, and learn from their experiences. With CLI commands, individuals can automate repetitive tasks, allowing them to allocate more time to learning and skill development. For instance, using CLI commands to provision infrastructure or deploy applications streamlines operations, freeing up resources for learning opportunities. Continuous learning in DevOps goes beyond acquiring new technical skills; it encompasses embracing a mindset of curiosity, adaptability, and collaboration. CLI commands play a crucial role in supporting this mindset by empowering individuals to explore new technologies, experiment with different configurations, and share knowledge with their peers. Collaboration is central to a culture of continuous learning in DevOps, and CLI commands facilitate collaboration by providing a common interface for teams to work together. Whether it's sharing scripts, automating workflows, or troubleshooting issues, CLI commands enable seamless communication and collaboration among team members. Moreover, CLI commands can be integrated with version control systems and collaboration platforms, allowing teams to share code snippets, track changes, and review each other's work efficiently. The iterative nature of DevOps encourages experimentation and continuous improvement, and CLI commands enable teams to iterate rapidly by automating repetitive tasks and deploying changes quickly. For example, using CLI commands to automate the testing and deployment of code enables teams to iterate on features and incorporate feedback from users more effectively. Additionally, CLI commands can be used to automate the collection of metrics and feedback, providing valuable insights into the effectiveness of development practices and facilitating continuous improvement. Continuous learning in DevOps extends beyond technical skills to include soft skills such as communication, collaboration, and problem-solving. CLI commands support the development of these skills by providing a platform for individuals to practice and refine their abilities in a hands-on manner. For instance, using CLI commands to automate deployments or troubleshoot issues encourages individuals to develop critical thinking skills and hone their problem-solving abilities. Furthermore, CLI commands can be used to *facilitate knowledge sharing and mentorship within teams, allowing less experienced members to learn from their more seasoned colleagues. In addition to supporting individual learning and development, CLI commands can also be used to foster a culture of knowledge sharing and collaboration across teams and departments. For example, using CLI commands to automate the creation of documentation or runbooks makes it easier for teams to share best practices, standardized procedures, and lessons learned. Moreover, CLI commands can be used to create reusable templates and scripts, enabling teams to leverage each other's expertise and avoid reinventing the wheel. Embracing a culture of continuous learning in DevOps requires organizations to provide the necessary resources and support for skill development. CLI commands can play a central role in this effort by providing a platform for self-directed learning and experimentation. For example, organizations can encourage employees to use CLI commands to explore new technologies, experiment with different configurations, and build prototypes. Additionally, organizations can provide access to training resources, online courses, and certification programs that incorporate CLI commands as part of the learning experience. Furthermore, organizations can create communities of practice and internal forums where employees can share knowledge,* collaborate on projects, and seek advice from their peers. As DevOps continues to evolve, organizations must prioritize continuous learning and skill development to remain competitive in the digital age. CLI commands offer a powerful tool for enabling this culture of learning by providing a platform for experimentation, collaboration, and skill development. By embracing CLI commands as part of their DevOps practices, organizations can empower their teams to adapt to change, innovate rapidly, and drive business success through continuous improvement.

Continuous improvement is a core principle of DevOps workflows, with CLI commands playing a pivotal role in facilitating this process by automating tasks, enabling rapid iteration, and providing valuable insights for optimization. CLI commands, such as those offered by popular DevOps tools like Azure DevOps, Git, Docker, and Kubernetes, empower teams to streamline their workflows, identify bottlenecks, and implement enhancements iteratively. For example, Git commands like "git commit" and "git push" allow developers to version control their codebase, enabling them to track changes, collaborate with teammates, and revert to previous versions if necessary. Similarly, Docker commands like "docker build" and "docker run" facilitate the creation and deployment of containerized applications, enabling teams to package their software in a consistent and portable manner. Kubernetes commands like "kubectl apply" and "kubectl scale" enable teams to manage containerized applications at scale, automating tasks such as deployment, scaling, and resource allocation. By leveraging these CLI commands, teams can establish a foundation for continuous improvement in their DevOps workflows. Continuous improvement in DevOps workflows involves a cyclical process of planning, implementing, measuring, and refining changes to enhance efficiency, reliability, and productivity. CLI commands provide the means to execute each phase of this process efficiently, enabling teams to iterate quickly and adapt to changing requirements. For instance, CLI commands can be used to automate routine tasks, such as provisioning infrastructure, configuring environments, and deploying applications, reducing the time and effort required for manual intervention. This automation not only accelerates the pace of development but also minimizes the risk of errors and inconsistencies, fostering a culture of reliability and predictability in DevOps workflows. Moreover, CLI commands can be used to collect and analyze data from various sources, such as logs, metrics, and user feedback, enabling teams to gain insights into the performance and usability of their applications. For example, Azure CLI commands like "az monitor metrics list" and "az monitor log query" allow teams to monitor the health and performance of their Azure resources in real-time, identifying issues and trends that may impact the user experience. Similarly, Git commands like "git log" and "git diff" provide visibility into the history and changes made to the codebase, facilitating collaboration and troubleshooting efforts. By leveraging these insights, teams can make informed decisions about where to focus their efforts for continuous improvement. In addition to automation and monitoring, CLI commands can also be used to implement proactive measures for enhancing security, compliance, and resilience in DevOps workflows. For example, Azure DevOps CLI commands like "az pipelines release approve" and "az pipelines release reject" enable teams to enforce approval gates and security checks before deploying changes to production, reducing the risk of unauthorized access or malicious activity. Similarly, Kubernetes commands like "kubectl rollout pause" and "kubectl rollout resume" allow teams to pause and resume deployments in response to security incidents or compliance violations, minimizing the impact on users and stakeholders. By integrating these security and compliance measures into their DevOps workflows, teams can mitigate risks and ensure the integrity and availability of their applications. Furthermore, CLI commands can be used to facilitate collaboration and communication among team members, stakeholders, and external partners, fostering a culture of transparency and accountability in DevOps workflows. For example, Git commands like "git merge" and "git pull request" enable developers to collaborate on code changes, review each other's work, and provide feedback in a structured and organized manner. Similarly, Docker commands like "docker push" and "docker pull" allow teams to share container images with external repositories, enabling seamless integration with third-party tools and services. By standardizing and automating these collaboration workflows, teams can reduce friction and delays in the development process, accelerating time-to-market and improving overall productivity. Continuous improvement in DevOps workflows requires a commitment to ongoing learning and experimentation, with CLI commands serving as the catalyst for innovation and evolution. For example, teams can use Azure CLI commands like "az extension add" and "az extension update" to install and update extensions that enhance the capabilities of their Azure DevOps environment, such as integration with third-party services or custom scripting. Similarly, Kubernetes commands like "kubectl apply -f" and "kubectl describe" allow teams to apply configuration changes and inspect resources in real-time, enabling them to experiment with different configurations *and iterate on their infrastructure and application design. By embracing a culture of experimentation and learning, teams can identify opportunities for optimization and refinement, driving continuous improvement in their DevOps workflows. In summary, CLI commands are essential tools for enabling continuous improvement in DevOps workflows, providing the means to automate tasks, monitor performance, enforce security, and facilitate collaboration. By leveraging these commands effectively, teams can iterate quickly, adapt to change, and deliver value to customers more efficiently.*

Chapter 10: Case Studies: Real-World Challenges and Solutions in DevOps

Analyzing real-world DevOps challenges reveals a complex landscape of obstacles and opportunities, with teams facing a myriad of issues spanning technical, cultural, and organizational domains. These challenges often arise from a combination of factors, including legacy systems, siloed teams, outdated processes, and resistance to change. In many cases, the transition to DevOps requires a fundamental shift in mindset and culture, with teams needing to embrace new ways of working, collaborating, and delivering value to customers. One common challenge faced by organizations embarking on their DevOps journey is the lack of alignment between development and operations teams, resulting in friction, inefficiencies, and delays in the delivery pipeline. This siloed mentality often stems from historical divisions of labor and responsibility, with developers focused on building features and operations teams focused on maintaining stability and uptime. Bridging this gap requires a cultural shift towards a more collaborative and cross-functional approach, with teams working together to streamline processes, share knowledge, and achieve common goals.

Another challenge is the complexity of modern software systems, which can involve multiple technologies, platforms, and dependencies. Managing this complexity requires robust automation, monitoring, and orchestration capabilities, along with strong governance and compliance measures to ensure consistency and reliability. Additionally, organizations may struggle with legacy systems and technical debt, which can hinder innovation and slow down the pace of delivery. Addressing these challenges often requires a combination of modernization efforts, refactoring legacy code, and adopting new tools and practices to improve agility and resilience. Furthermore, organizations may face challenges related to tooling and infrastructure, with disparate systems, manual processes, and lack of integration hindering productivity and collaboration. Consolidating tools, automating repetitive tasks, and standardizing workflows can help streamline operations and improve efficiency across the development lifecycle. Moreover, organizations must navigate the complexities of compliance and security in a rapidly evolving threat landscape, with stringent regulations and industry standards imposing strict requirements on data privacy, access controls, and risk management. Implementing robust security controls, conducting regular audits, and integrating security into the development lifecycle are essential *for ensuring compliance and mitigating risk. Another challenge is managing the scale and complexity of cloud-native architectures, which can involve thousands of microservices, containers, and serverless functions distributed across hybrid and multi-cloud environments. This distributed nature introduces new challenges related to monitoring, observability, and troubleshooting, with teams needing to adopt new tools and practices to gain visibility and control over their infrastructure and applications. Additionally, organizations may face challenges related to cultural resistance and change management, with employees accustomed to traditional ways of working reluctant to embrace DevOps practices and principles. Overcoming this resistance requires strong leadership, effective communication, and a commitment to continuous learning and improvement. In summary, analyzing real-world DevOps challenges reveals a diverse array of obstacles and opportunities, with teams needing to navigate technical, cultural, and organizational complexities to succeed in their transformation journey. By addressing these challenges systematically and collaboratively, organizations can unlock the full potential of DevOps and deliver value to customers more efficiently and effectively. Examining case studies of successful DevOps implementations and solutions provides valuable insights into the strategies, practices, and outcomes that have led to tangible business benefits for organizations across various industries. One such case study is the transformation journey of a global e-commerce company that faced challenges with frequent outages, slow time-to-market, and high operational costs. By adopting DevOps principles and practices, including infrastructure as code (IaC), continuous integration (CI), and continuous delivery (CD), the company was able to improve system reliability, accelerate release cycles, and reduce infrastructure provisioning time from weeks to minutes. They achieved this by automating manual processes, implementing robust monitoring and alerting systems, and fostering a culture of collaboration and experimentation among development and operations teams. As a result, the company saw a significant reduction in downtime, an increase in customer satisfaction, and a substantial decrease in infrastructure costs. Another compelling case study is the transformation of a leading financial services organization that struggled with siloed teams, legacy systems, and regulatory compliance challenges. By adopting DevOps practices, such as version control, automated testing, and deployment automation, the organization was able to streamline their development and release processes, improve code quality, and ensure regulatory compliance. They achieved this by implementing a centralized version control system, integrating automated testing into their CI/CD pipelines, and establishing robust change management processes. As a result, the organization saw a marked improvement in software quality, a reduction in compliance-related incidents, and an increase in developer productivity. Additionally, a case study of a healthcare provider illustrates how DevOps principles and practices can enable organizations to deliver innovative solutions while maintaining compliance with strict regulatory requirements. By embracing automation, continuous monitoring, and security best practices, the organization was able to accelerate the delivery of new features and services while ensuring the confidentiality, integrity, and availability of patient data. They accomplished this by implementing a secure software development lifecycle (SDLC), conducting regular security assessments, and leveraging cloud-native security controls. As a result, the organization saw improved patient outcomes, increased operational efficiency, and enhanced regulatory compliance. Furthermore, a case study of a technology startup showcases the transformative impact of DevOps on product innovation and market competitiveness. By adopting agile methodologies, cloud-native architectures, and DevOps practices, the startup was able to rapidly iterate on their product offerings, scale their infrastructure, and respond quickly to changing customer needs. They achieved this by leveraging cloud services such as AWS and Azure, implementing automated testing and deployment pipelines, and fostering a culture of experimentation and learning. As a result, the startup saw accelerated time-to-market, increased customer adoption, and sustained business growth. In summary, case studies of successful DevOps implementations and solutions demonstrate the transformative power of DevOps in driving business agility, innovation, and competitive advantage. By embracing DevOps principles and practices, organizations can overcome challenges, accelerate delivery, and deliver value to customers more effectively and efficiently.*

Conclusion

In summary, the book bundle "Azure DevOps Engineer: Exam AZ-400 - Designing and Implementing Microsoft DevOps Solutions" offers a comprehensive journey through the world of Azure DevOps, catering to individuals at all skill levels, from beginners to experts. Through the four books included in this bundle, readers have been equipped with the necessary knowledge and skills to excel in the field of DevOps and effectively tackle the challenges presented by the AZ-400 exam.

In "Azure DevOps Fundamentals: A Beginner's Guide to Exam AZ-400," readers were introduced to the foundational concepts of Azure DevOps, laying the groundwork for their understanding of DevOps principles, practices, and tools. This book provided a solid starting point for individuals new to Azure DevOps, offering clear explanations and practical examples to facilitate learning.

"Mastering Continuous Integration and Continuous Deployment with Azure DevOps: Exam AZ-400" delved deeper into the realm of CI/CD pipelines, guiding readers through the intricacies of automating the software delivery process using

Azure DevOps. By mastering CI/CD techniques, readers gained the ability to streamline development workflows, increase deployment frequency, and improve overall software quality.

"Advanced Azure DevOps Techniques: Architecting for Scalability and Resilience - Exam AZ-400" elevated readers' understanding of Azure DevOps to the next level by exploring advanced topics such as scalability, resilience, and architectural patterns. Through real-world case studies and practical examples, readers learned how to design and implement robust DevOps solutions capable of meeting the demands of modern, cloud-native applications.

Finally, "DevOps Expert: Achieving Mastery in Azure DevOps and Beyond - Exam AZ-400" served as the ultimate guide for individuals seeking to become true experts in Azure DevOps. Covering a wide range of topics, from security and compliance to advanced monitoring and analytics, this book empowered readers to tackle complex challenges with confidence and proficiency.

Together, these four books provide a comprehensive roadmap for individuals aspiring to become Azure DevOps engineers, equipping them with the knowledge, skills, and strategies needed to succeed *in today's fast-paced, technology-driven world. Whether readers are preparing for the AZ-400 exam or striving to excel in their careers, this book bundle serves as an invaluable resource, guiding them every step of the way on their DevOps journey.*

www.ingramcontent.com/pod-product-compliance
Lightning Source LLC
Chambersburg PA
CBHW070935050326
40689CB00014B/3213